The U.S. Constitution in Five Minutes

The U.S. Constitution in Five Minutes

Edited by
Joseph L. Smith and David E. Klein

eQuinox

SHEFFIELD UK   BRISTOL CT

Published by Equinox Publishing Ltd.

UK: Office 415, The Workstation, 15 Paternoster Row, Sheffield, South Yorkshire S1 2BX

USA: ISD, 70 Enterprise Drive, Bristol, CT 06010

www.equinoxpub.com

First published 2023

British Library Cataloguing-in-Publication Data

A catalogue record for this book is available from the British Library.

ISBN-13   978 1 80050 284 0   (hardback)
          978 1 80050 285 7   (paperback)
          978 1 80050 286 4   (ePDF)
          978 1 80050 350 2   (ePub)

Library of Congress Cataloging-in-Publication Data

Names: Smith, Joseph L., editor. | Klein, David, editor.
Title: The U.S. Constitution in five minutes / edited by Joseph L. Smith and David Klein.
Other titles: US Constitution in five minutes
Description: Bristol : Equinox Publishing Ltd, 2023. | Includes bibliographical references and index. | Summary: "The U.S. Constitution in Five Minutes presents 59 essays on subjects central to the meaning and application of the Constitution. Intended for anyone who wants a deeper understanding of the underlying principles of the U.S. political system, the book will also be a valuable supplement to political science courses. As with all the "in 5 Minutes" books, the essays are written in lively and accessible prose and are brief enough to be read in five minutes"-- Provided by publisher.
Identifiers: LCCN 2022048593 (print) | LCCN 2022048594 (ebook) | ISBN 9781800502840 (hardback) | ISBN 9781800502857 (paperback) | ISBN 9781800502864 (pdf) | ISBN 9781800503502 (epub)
Subjects: LCSH: Constitutional law--United States. | Constitutions—United States.
Classification: LCC KF4550 .U79 2023 (print) | LCC KF4550 (ebook) | DDC 342.73--dc23/eng/20230223
LC record available at https://lccn.loc.gov/2022048593
LC ebook record available at https://lccn.loc.gov/2022048594

Typeset by Scribe Inc.

Contents

Individual Liberties

Preface

Joseph L. Smith and David E. Klein

Considering that it has the job of structuring and guiding an entire twenty-first-century political system, the U.S. Constitution is strikingly—even shockingly—short and old. You have probably accepted (without reading them) software user license agreements that are longer than the Constitution, even counting its amendments. And even counting the amendments, most of the Constitution dates to long before the invention of the electric light, cars, and planes, let alone computers, cell phones, and the internet.

At the time the Constitution was written, the United States was fairly small and weak, and the new national government was not expected to play a major role in either international affairs or the daily lives of its citizens. The framers knew the country would grow, but even if they could have conceived of an area almost equal to all of Europe's and a population of more than three hundred million, they could not have imagined how vast and powerful the United States would become in economic and military terms. Nor could they have imagined how the scope of government (throughout the world) would grow as people demanded more support for health, education, environmental protection, income maintenance, and consumer protection. Concepts like freedom and equality were important to the framers' thinking, but our understandings of the meaning and scope of these concepts have changed dramatically.

What are we to make of a brief document written in mostly general terms by people who could not possibly foresee how much society and the role of government in society would change in 250 years? It is easy to imagine such a document being reduced to a meaningless symbol, largely forgotten or ignored. But in fact, the Constitution has retained a central presence in U.S. politics. Naturally, much of the everyday business of government and politics is conducted without conscious thought about the Constitution. But it is always there in the background, guiding and constraining officials' behavior and choices. Activists on any issue will seek to show that their position is more consistent than their opponents' with the words and values of the Constitution. And an accusation of unconstitutionality is one of the most damning that can be leveled against any law or governmental action.

The Constitution's centrality to political criticism and justification results in lively debates not only about the meaning of certain provisions of the Constitution but even about how those meanings should be discerned, and by whom. What are the Constitution's guiding principles? When interpreting specific provisions, should we foster constitutional stability by viewing them in the context of the times in which they were written, or should our interpretations reflect today's norms and understandings? When certain principles or provisions of the Constitution conflict with others, which should prevail? Should questions of this sort be answered by the courts, by elected officials, or even by the people themselves?

These layers of controversy appear and reappear throughout the book. Specific provisions and problems dominate the middle sections of the book, while it begins and ends with broader themes: the historical roots and fundamental choices of the Constitution in the opening essays and the Constitution's effectiveness and comparisons with other countries' constitutions in the final essays. But as you will see, broader and narrower questions always become entangled, just like questions of what, how, and who.

Not one of the questions addressed in this book can be fully answered in a brief essay, and no essay presumes to offer the final word on a topic or tell you what to think about it. Of course, we hope you will learn new facts and gain a clearer understanding as you move through the book, whether you start at the beginning or with whatever essay grabs your eye. But just as importantly, we hope you will experience the excitement of seeing familiar issues in new ways and being drawn into debates that had previously escaped your attention.

Note on internet sources for further reading: the essays in this volume cite numerous Supreme Court cases and essays from *The Federalist Papers*. All of these can be found on the internet. We recommend the following sites as especially easy to navigate and read. For Supreme Court opinions, we recommend Google Scholar (https://scholar.google.com, click the "Case law" button below the search box), Justia.com (https://supreme .justia.com), or Cornell University's Legal Information Institute (https:// www.law.cornell.edu/supremecourt/text). Google scholar provides only the text of the opinions; the latter two sites provide context as well. For *The Federalist Papers*, we like the Library of Congress site (https://guides.loc .gov/federalist-papers/full-text).

Joseph L. Smith   David E. Klein
The University of Alabama   Eastern Michigan University

Origins

1
Why Do We Have a Constitution?

James Todd

> We the People of the United States, in Order to form a more
> perfect Union, establish Justice, insure domestic Tranquility,
> provide for the common defence, promote the general Welfare,
> and secure the Blessings of Liberty to ourselves and our Pos-
> terity, do ordain and establish this Constitution for the United
> States of America.
>
> —U.S. Constitution, Preamble

Since you are reading this, you are probably interested in politics—the
debates and characters in American government. For political junkies,
following the races and actions of the government can be exciting at times
and infuriating at others. However, our governmental processes happen
only because of the Constitution.

A constitution is a set of fundamental laws and principles that work
together to create a governmental system. A constitution is a creative thing
because it brings the government into existence. A constitution's laws are
fundamental because they are the basic rules for how ordinary laws
are made and enforced by the government.

The U.S. Constitution, like any constitution, brings a unique system
of government to life. In a one-sentence preamble (quoted above), seven
articles, and twenty-seven amendments, the national government of the
United States is created, shaped, empowered, and limited, and the governments of states are limited as well. This Constitution ultimately declares
itself "the supreme Law of the Land."

Importantly, the Constitution puts requirements into place that
reflect higher principles, values, and goals. Many of the values advanced
by the Constitution reflect the earliest experience of the American nation:
the Revolutionary War (1775–83), the Declaration of Independence

from British rule (1776), and America's first constitution, the Articles of Confederation (1781–89).

The group of people who wrote the American Constitution in 1787, often referred to as the framers, derived important principles from these experiences. They had a clear preference for a government that was created by a constitution, or the principle of constitutionalism. Without a constitution, the goals of the governmental system would not likely be realized. The government would instead be lawless. Also, they saw the advantage of a *written* constitution that could be understood by the public and by officials in government.

The framers wanted a republic, or a government run by the people's representatives. They believed that self-government was essential to freedom; consent-based government is a value asserted in the Declaration of Independence. The government created by the Constitution reflects the principle of self-government in many different places and even at times *democratic* self-government. Through later changes, America's republic became even more democratic than the framers originally envisioned.

The framers believed in the value of human liberty. This belief shows up in the Declaration of Independence. This principle is advanced by any constitutional requirement that limits governmental power. In time, a series of ten amendments called the Bill of Rights (1791) was added to the Constitution to codify Americans' basic rights and to limit national power. In later amendments, especially the Fourteenth Amendment, the principle of liberty was extended far beyond the terms of the original Constitution, which had made notorious accommodations for slavery and had done little to protect freedom from state power.

Despite the Declaration's claim that "all men are created equal," the framers did not enshrine any guarantee of equality in the Constitution. Equal protection of the law would become a constitutional principle only after the Civil War and the abolition of slavery (by constitutional amendment). In light of this history, equality now stands as one of today's most debated constitutional principles.

Because of the weaknesses of the Articles of Confederation, most framers agreed on a stronger national government. The vast American domain needed a single government, supreme over the states, that could handle national challenges and objectives. The framers had to fashion a constitution that strengthened the national government but did not allow the national government to dominate the states. The Constitution manages to balance these two levels of government. In general, the Constitution empowers the national government and limits the power of states to protect important national objectives, including commerce, war, and diplomacy. In later amendments, civil rights, voting rights, and equal protection of law also became national objectives.

The Constitution's preamble reads as a statement of ultimate principles. The overall purposes of the system of government created by the Constitution are made plain—yet another benefit of a written constitution. These purposes all in some way trace to republicanism, rights protection, or governmental strength.

The opening words, "We the People," indicate that a popular basis is the only legitimate basis for a constitution; in republican thought, constitutions should not be imposed on a people. If they are imposed, the governing arrangements will not likely meet the people's needs or embody their basic principles.

The preamble is clear that the relevant people are those "of the United States." The document boldly claims to speak for everyone in all states. These people of the United States are united for the first time under the Constitution's requirements of popular representation, a single executive, a national judicial system, and other shared institutions.

The preamble articulates the goal of creating "a more perfect union"—a more complete union of people and states than had prevailed at any earlier time. The new national government is to be powerful enough to "insure domestic tranquility," "provide for the common defence," and "promote the general welfare." These objectives were not met under the Articles of Confederation, which explains the Constitution's emphasis on national strength and supremacy.

Not to be overlooked in all this talk about government strength, however, are other important values. The preamble reminds us that government—any government—uses its power not for its own sake but instead to "secure the blessings of liberty" and to "establish justice." The institutions of the new government have significant powers but not total power. They are limited by the very existence of a constitution and by its deliberate arrangements. They provide national order and harmony only so that people have a chance to live in conditions of freedom and justice.

Lastly, the Constitution's amendment process furthers the long-term vision of the preamble, one of secure liberty for "posterity." The Constitution provides for the means of its own change, but these means require true nationwide agreement, or else the fundamental law will come to resemble ordinary law. Thus, the Constitution can improve without ceasing to be one.

About the author

James Todd is an associate professor of politics at Palm Beach Atlantic University. His work focuses on U.S. constitutionalism and the Supreme Court.

Suggestions for further reading

In this book
See essays 2 (Who Wrote the Constitution?), 3 (Human Nature and the Constitution), and 5 (Emulation and Innovation in the Constitutional System).

Elsewhere
Amar, Akhil Reed. 2005. *America's Constitution: A Biography*. New York: Random House.

Beeman, Richard. 2009. *Plain, Honest Men: The Making of the American Constitution*. New York: Random House.

National Constitution Center. http://www.nationalconstitutioncenter.org—Federally chartered website with historical and current materials related to the Constitution.

2
Who Wrote the Constitution?

Madison Shanks and Kirk A. Randazzo

When people think about the beginning of the United States and the drafting of the Constitution, they often refer to the "Founding Fathers" or the "framers" as a single collection of individuals. Additionally, they often use these terms interchangeably even though they refer to different groups (with some overlap). For example, Thomas Jefferson contributed to the independence of the United States and therefore is one of the Founding Fathers. However, Jefferson is not one of the framers of the Constitution; he served as ambassador to France during the convention in 1787 and did not attend the sessions in Philadelphia. This essay focuses on the individuals who were active in creating the U.S. Constitution (the framers) and explores the competing tensions through which the framers worked to develop a new foundation of government in the United States. As Benjamin Franklin observed in September 1787, "When you assemble a number of men to have the advantage of their joint wisdom, you inevitably assemble with those men, all their prejudices, their passions, their errors of opinion, their local interests, and their selfish views." While there were several competing tensions among the framers, this essay focuses on two of the most dominant: (a) between large states and small states and (b) across economic interests.

When speaking of the framers, one needs to begin the examination with James Madison. Though small in stature, Madison played a large role at the convention, and he is widely considered the "Father of the Constitution." Previously, he drafted Virginia's state constitution, and this served as the template for the U.S. Constitution. Madison was also prominent in crafting the Virginia plan for a bicameral legislature with both chambers based on proportional representation. Congressional representation was one of the key tensions among the framers, but beyond the debate over representation, Madison's work on the Virginia plan helped broaden the conversations toward the structure of government and the balance of powers. While Madison knew the federal government needed more centralized power than it had under the Articles of Confederation, his broader goal was to shift the debate toward a compromise that shared sovereignty between the states and the federal government. While Madison worked on a grander scale with the premise and underlying ideals of the Constitution, a total of fifty-five delegates attended the Constitutional Convention, many of whom are little known but nonetheless played crucial roles in getting the Constitution drafted. Madison's ideal of shared sovereignty manifested practically in a question of representation with disagreements between large and small states. Large states (like Madison's home state of Virginia) wanted the legislature to be determined based on population, which would give these states more power in legislating. In contrast, smaller states (such as New Jersey) argued for equal representation regardless of population.

Edmund Randolph actually proposed the Virginia plan. In response, William Paterson proposed the New Jersey plan for a unicameral legislature with equal representation that would protect the interests of smaller states from domination. The convention quickly reached an impasse between these two proposals. Roger Sherman and Oliver Ellsworth then proposed the Connecticut Compromise that retained a bicameral legislature with the lower chamber employing proportional representation and the upper chamber having equal representation. This compromise was ultimately approved by the delegates, with Elbridge Gerry casting the deciding vote in favor. Ironically, Gerry was one of only three delegates present at the signing to not endorse the new Constitution, citing his disapproval because the document did not contain a Bill of Rights.

With the matter of representation settled, the delegates turned their attention to other important issues, which allowed different tensions to emerge. One of these cleavages involved commerce and the degree of federal regulation over economic interests. A key figure in these debates was Alexander Hamilton, who argued in favor of a strong federal government that could promote economic stability. During these debates, the issue of slavery became prominent. States that were more self-sufficient with enslaved agrarian labor were reluctant to endorse the federal government taking on debt from the more industrial states. In contrast, the more industrial states argued in favor of debt sharing because of the increased access to credit and greater financial stability.

For many delegates, their personal opinions of slavery were of less concern than the cleavages between industrial versus agricultural economies and the broader goal of achieving agreement on a constitution that could be ratified. For instance, several of Maryland's delegates supported the industrial interests of a strong central government for taxation purposes despite holding slaves themselves. Conversely, while New Jersey delegate William Livingston was especially opposed to slavery in his personal life, he was key in drafting the three-fifths compromise to ensure slave states would ratify the Constitution.

A final, and more abstract, question during the convention involved delineating between federal and state authority. Daniel Carroll, along with James Wilson, contributed two important pieces to the Constitution by addressing this question. First, Carroll proposed a shift of power from the legislature to the people via direct election of the president. Second, he proposed limiting the federal government's authority by declaring that all powers not explicitly enumerated in the Constitution remain with states.

The convention lasted from May until September 1787, when the final task of condensing the twenty-three resolutions proposed during the convention down to only seven articles fell to Gouverneur Morris. He spoke more than anyone else during the convention—a total of 173 times—and gained the title "Penman of the Constitution" due to the tact with which he crafted the document.

Though we often think of the framers as a single group, the reality is much more complex. Each delegate represented the interests of his state, and these tensions—over representation and the regulation of economic interests (including slavery)—led to several compromises that serve as the foundation of the U.S. Constitution.

About the authors

Madison Shanks is a PhD candidate in political science at the University of South Carolina. Her work focuses on attorney strategy in criminal cases at the U.S. Federal District Courts.

Kirk A. Randazzo is a professor and chair of the Department of Political Science at the University of South Carolina. His research focuses on constraints to judicial behavior, the balance between liberty and security in foreign policy litigation, and the role of courts in democratic consolidation.

Suggestions for further reading

In this book
See essays 1 (Why Do We Have a Constitution?) and 3 (Human Nature and the Constitution).

Elsewhere

Klarman, Michael J. 2016. *The Framers' Coup: The Making of the United States Constitution*. New York: Oxford University Press.

Teaching American History. https://teachingamericanhistory.org/resource/the-constitutional-convention-refurbished/—Website with teaching materials related to the Constitutional Convention.

3
Human Nature and the Constitution

David Lay Williams

As this book demonstrates in so many ways, the U.S. Constitution is among the most debated documents in American life. And like other debates about contested concepts, such as religion, these debates often require returning to their founding documents. For constitutional scholars, this means returning not only to the Constitution itself but to the debates surrounding its ratification from 1787 to 1789. Most centrally, this means examining the essays published by the proposed Constitution's advocates and critics. The most important defenders of the Constitution in this period—Alexander Hamilton, James Madison, and John Jay—published a series of eighty-five essays published in New York newspapers in order to urge New Yorkers to vote for ratification. These essays have come to be called *The Federalist* (or sometimes, *The Federalist Papers*). The Constitution's opponents eventually were called, intuitively, the Anti-Federalists. Collectively, *The Federalist* and the Anti-Federalist essays have assumed the status of not only the most important assessments of the Constitution but also some of the most important American writings on political theory more generally.

Among the most important divisions between the Federalists and Anti-Federalists was the question of human nature itself. Are people good or bad by nature? For many, the Christian doctrine of original sin—the theory that all of humanity is inherently wicked—was decisive. But it was also the case that philosophers in the eighteenth century, especially the Genevan Jean-Jacques Rousseau (1712–78), began to challenge this received view. There is evidence of both views in the founding documents. One of the great Anti-Federalists, Brutus, argued that "it is a truth confirmed by the unerring experience of the ages, that every man, and every body of men, invested with power, are ever disposed to increase it, and to acquire a superiority over every thing that stands in their way." For him, it is a fundamental principle of human nature that "every individual pursues his own interest."

For Brutus and others among the Anti-Federalists, this view of human nature has important implications for governance. From a historical perspective, they were particularly concerned about what they considered to be a major failing of the British constitutional system—an excessive degree of power residing in a centralized monarch. For them, it is the nature of excessively concentrated power to tyrannize, which is why they had separated from Britain in the first place. This meant, for the Anti-Federalists, that government needed to be kept on a short leash, since its tendency is to expand and then tyrannize. This could be achieved, they argued, by keeping centers of power closer to the people—by making state and local government sovereign, since the people could better supervise power closer to home. It also meant shorter terms of office. Brutus, for example, favored four-year terms for senators and was deeply skeptical of life terms for federal judges. In both instances, he argued, federal government officials—insofar as they were necessary—would be watched jealously by the people, who would rightly worry about the abuse of power.

The Federalists shared some of the Anti-Federalist skepticism with regard to human nature. In *Federalist* no. 48, James Madison conceded that "power is of an encroaching nature." He would famously elaborate in *Federalist* no. 51, "If men were angels, no government would be necessary." Less known, but perhaps even more damning of human nature, Alexander Hamilton wrote in *Federalist* no. 6 that "men are ambitious, vindictive, and rapacious." To this extent, *The Federalist* argues for many controls on government—including the celebrated checks and balances embedded in the constitutional system, such as bicameralism, the presidential veto, judicial review, and even impeachment. These checks were created to address the concern that one branch or another might be tempted to abuse its power, given this account of human nature.

Yet some of *The Federalist* essays offer a more nuanced account of human nature. Madison writes in *Federalist* no. 55, "As there is a degree of depravity in mankind which requires a certain degree of circumspection and distrust, so there are other qualities in human nature which justify a certain portion of esteem and confidence. Republican government presupposes the existence of these qualities in a higher degree than any other form." Similarly, in *Federalist* no. 76, Hamilton observes, "This supposition of universal venality in human nature is little less an error in political reasoning, than the supposition of universal rectitude. The institution of delegated power implies, that there is a portion of virtue and honor among mankind, which may be a reasonable foundation of confidence; and experience justifies the theory. Civic virtue has been found to exist even in the most corrupt periods of the most corrupt governments."

WILLIAMS—HUMAN NATURE AND THE CONSTITUTION   13

The implication of passages like these distinguishes the Federalists from their opponents. Whereas the Anti-Federalists largely imply that one can *never* sleep on a thoroughly corrupted human nature, drawing here from the Baron de Montesquieu, the Federalists imply that republicanism—their preferred name for the theory of government underlying the Constitution, a system in which voters oriented to the common good elect leaders to exercise power on their behalf—requires sometimes trusting in human nature to do the right thing, even when wielding political power, so long as there is a foundation of civic virtue to be found in the populace capable of choosing virtuous leaders. For example, for them, we should be able to trust senators with six-year terms or federal judges with life terms. It means that even though some elements of the government might be tempted to abuse power, other branches and agents can be counted on to act on higher motives and call the government itself to account for potential abuses. Maybe most importantly, it means that the presence of a powerful central government—at some distance from the people it serves—is not necessarily a menace but rather potentially a force for justice and the common good.

About the author

David Lay Williams is a professor of political science at DePaul University. His research addresses issues in the history of political thought, especially during the eighteenth century.

Suggestions for further reading

In this book
See essays 4 (Racism in the Constitution), 5 (Emulation and Innovation in the Constitutional System), and 26 (Term Lengths, Stability, and Responsiveness).

Elsewhere
Brutus. 2003. Letters 1 (pp. 437–47), 2 (pp. 447–53), 5 (pp. 465–72) and 11 (pp. 501–6). In *The Federalist with the Letters of "Brutus,"* edited by Terrence Ball. Cambridge, UK: Cambridge University Press.

The Federalist Papers nos. 6, 10, 48, 51, 55, and 76.

Montesquieu, Charles. 1989. Sections 4.5 (pp. 35–36), 5.3 (pp. 43–44), and 8.16 (p. 124). In *The Spirit of the Laws*, edited by Anne Cohler, Baisa Miller, and Harold Stone. Cambridge, UK: Cambridge University Press.

4

Racism in the Constitution

Leslie F. Goldstein

While both the body of the Constitution (ratified in 1788) and its first set of amendments (ratified in 1791) might look to the naked eye like proequality documents, historical context and official interpretation tell a different story.

The original Constitution does contain a number of explicit protections of liberty and equality. At both the state and federal levels, titles of nobility are prohibited, trials by jury are guaranteed, and bills of attainder (legislative declarations of punishment without judicial trial) are forbidden, as are ex post facto laws (those that punish persons later for actions that are innocent at the time; art. I, sec. 9 and 10; art. III, sec. 2, cl. 3). And the Fifth Amendment states with apparent clarity, "No person shall be deprived of life, *liberty*, or property [emphasis added] without due process of law."

However, at the time the Constitution was adopted, the lawbooks in every state in the union contained racially discriminatory statutes. And the earliest congresses did not lag far behind. Congress limited naturalization for citizenship to "whites" (1790) and specified white male citizens aged eighteen to forty-five as the group required to register for the national militia (1792). In 1810, Congress prohibited Blacks from being hired as postal carriers. In 1812, Congress authorized the government of the District of Columbia "to restrain and prohibit the nightly and other disorderly meetings of slaves, free negroes [*sic*] and mulattoes, and to punish such slaves by whipping." So while it might seem obvious to us that a law denying an entire racial group the liberty of being hired for a job, meeting with friends at night, or becoming a U.S. citizen *does* deprive someone of liberty without due process of law, the dominant legal understanding prior to the Civil War did not read the Constitution this way.

Moreover, while the authors of the U.S. Constitution (at least according to James Madison's notes on the Constitutional Convention) took care to keep the words "slave" and "slavery" out of the Constitution so as not to authoritatively institutionalize the practice, three clauses in the document notoriously compromised with supporters of slavery. First, Congress was forbidden to ban the foreign import of slaves for at least twenty years. (At 12:01 a.m. on the first day permitted, Congress did ban the practice.) Second, the population-based formula for states' congressional representation, instead of fully counting slaves in the population (as was desired by the slave states) or not counting them at all (as was desired by the nonslave states), counted them as three-fifths of a person. Third, states were forbidden to legislate to free "persons held to service or labor [under laws] in one state, escaping into another" but instead were told to "deliver up" such persons "on claim of the party to whom such service or labor may be due" (art. IV, sec. 2, cl. 2, 3).

By the 1830s, a split developed among abolitionists over how to interpret this collection of clauses: William Lloyd Garrison, Wendell Phillips, and others condemned the Constitution as a compact with hell and said the North must secede to rid itself of slavery. William Goodell, Gerrit Smith, Frederick Douglass, and others pointed to the proequality and proliberty clauses in the Constitution and urged that the document, properly interpreted, would and should ban slavery and other racial discrimination. The Republican Party emerged from the latter group in the 1850s to argue that slavery must be banned in all jurisdictions under federal authority, including any territories. This posture provoked the South into secession and the Civil War, which then provoked the Republican Party to a more radical posture, such that slavery was altogether banned in the Thirteenth Amendment (1865), racial discrimination banned in the Fourteenth Amendment (1868), and racial discrimination specifically in voter eligibility banned in the Fifteenth Amendment (1870).

Whereas the U.S. Constitution does not *explicitly* discriminate between persons of sub-Saharan African descent ("Blacks") and persons of European descent ("whites"), it does single out peoples indigenous to America ("Indians"). Peoples native to this continent were viewed as conquered but mostly autonomous. Thus, Article I specifies that Congress shall have power "to regulate commerce with foreign nations . . . and with the Indian Tribes." As late as 1870, treaties were made with native tribes as if they were sovereign foreign countries. Over time, all Native Americans were granted U.S. citizenship, but this process was not completed until 1924.

Governmental policy toward the tribes has sometimes been purposely harsh, sometimes benign, and often a mix. On paper, treatment of the tribes often appeared benign. Noted legal scholar Felix Cohen pointed out that even the horrific (in practice) Indian Removal Act of the 1830s–40s involved purchases from Indian tribes of virtually every acre in contrast to the policies on treatment of Indigenous property in South America, Canada, and Australia. The United States, for instance, having paid Napoleon fifteen million dollars for the right to rule the Louisiana Territory, then paid the Native Americans three hundred million dollars for that property (exclusive of the cessions for tribal reservations). Even policies meant to be benign have sometimes had harsh, unintended consequences. Native peoples in the United States remain for the most part extremely disadvantaged, although there are many notable exceptions, at both the individual and tribal levels.

About the author

Leslie F. Goldstein is the Judge Hugh M. Morris Professor Emerita of political science at the University of Delaware. Her primary research interests are in the fields of constitutional law and political philosophy, especially the intersection of these fields and the rights of women and racial minorities.

Suggestions for further reading

In this book
See essays 2 (Who Wrote the Constitution?), 40 (How Did the Civil War Amendments Change the Constitution?), 43 (Does the Equal Protection Clause Cover Gender?), and 45 (Regulating Private Discrimination).

Elsewhere
Cohen, Felix. 1947. "Original Indian Title." *Minnesota Law Review* 32:29–58.

Goldstein, Leslie F. 2017. *The U.S. Supreme Court and Racial Minorities: Two Centuries of Judicial Review on Trial.* Cheltenham: Edward Elgar Publishing.

Litwack, Leon. 1961. *North of Slavery.* Chicago: University of Chicago Press.

5
Emulation and Innovation in the Constitutional System

A. K. Shauku

The architecture of the U.S. constitutional system is a mix of elements drawn from the British tradition with adaptations to the needs of a developing political community in North America. In 1776, representatives of the thirteen British colonies in North America declared each colony "free and independent states" and insisted that "each state retains its sovereignty, freedom, and independence" even as they endeavored to "enter into a firm league of friendship with each other." Thus, the new states initially sought the benefits of political *alliance* but not full political integration under a common government. Indeed, a congress consisting of recallable delegates from each state was established, but it operated more as an instrument for building consensus *among* the several state governments than a governing institution *over* them. This initial posture provides context for the series of compromises that follow.

After war with the British concluded in 1783 and the external threat was removed, cooperation among the states began to fray. A Constitutional Convention was convened in 1787 to reimagine the "league of friendship" into a more sustainable union. Greater political integration was seen as the key. Three new institutions emerged from the convention—a bicameral congress, a presidency, and a Supreme Court—that differed from the original congress in two significant respects. First, the new institutions would not merely constitute a set of arrangements between state governments but would have some connection to the population at large. Second, the new national institutions would have some authority *over* the states. This arrangement—known as federalism—which divided governmental power and responsibility between a central government and regional governments, preserved some of the independence of each state while requiring greater coordination. This balance of independence and coordination too proved unstable. The question of whether slavery would be allowed to continue in existing states and allowed in new states ultimately led to a civil war. Several amendments to the Constitution have attempted to clarify the scope of authority granted to the national government and that reserved to the states, but the federal relationship continues to generate conflict and be refined through legislation and litigation.

Bicameral—that is, two-chambered—legislatures were not new. The British Parliament consisted of two distinct bodies, the House of Commons and the House of Lords. While members of the former body were popularly elected by district, members of the latter occupied appointed and hereditary seats, representing the interests of the landed class. In the American context, bicameralism also balanced distinct societal interests. The legislature created under Article I of the Constitution established a House of Representatives and a Senate. Members of the House—elected by small, popular constituencies for two-year terms—were intended to be directly responsive to ordinary citizens. Members of the Senate, selected by state legislatures (until altered by the Seventeenth Amendment) for six-year terms, were intended to represent the states as distinct political entities and check popular impulses. Each state, no matter its population, was represented by two senators, but a state's number of representatives in the House was based on its population. Because the two chambers must agree in order to enact legislation, this form of representation implies that policies must garner the support of a majority of the voting public and a majority of the states as individual political communities.

Distrust of the executive was another feature of the British political tradition, which influenced the American founders. In Britain, the power of the chief executive, the monarch, was gradually eroded in favor of the legislature. By the time of the American Revolution, the power of the British monarch was significantly circumscribed. Eventually, the monarchy would shrink to a ceremonial role, and the legislature would select an executive from among its own ranks, which held office at the pleasure of the legislature. In postrevolutionary North America, the states experimented with all-powerful legislatures and found them unsatisfactory for a host of reasons, including a lack of decisiveness. By the time of the 1787 convention, delegates had soured on unchecked legislatures, and Madison cautioned against "a tendency in our governments to throw all power into the legislative vortex." Instead, Article II of the Constitution provides for a presidency with an independent electoral mandate and such powers as appointment, treaty-making, direction of the military, and the granting of pardons—although only the last of these powers does the president exercise with a free hand. The president was also provided a direct role in legislation—the veto—to serve as a last check against unwise legislation.

The judiciary that emerged from the convention was the most underspecified of the three new institutions. Article III of the Constitution provides for "one Supreme Court" and "such inferior courts as the Congress may . . . ordain and establish" but tells us neither the number of judges to serve on these courts nor the qualifications for office and virtually nothing pertaining to the courts' internal procedures. This lack of specification can be partly attributed to the time and effort already spent by convention delegates on the first two branches. Perhaps the branch dubbed by Alexander Hamilton as "least dangerous" could be safely left to subsequent congressional design. But this relative absent-mindedness with respect to the third branch of national government is owed at least in part to the sense among the framers that the function of courts within the Anglo-American political tradition was already well understood and uncontroversial. The irony here is that the Supreme Court, in *Marbury v. Madison* (1803), would assume for itself the power of constitutional judicial review ("If an act of the legislature . . . be in opposition to the constitution . . . disregarding the law . . . is the very essence of judicial duty"), a considerable departure.

In all, the architecture of the constitutional system—with features such as federalism, bicameralism, an independent executive, and judiciary—reflects both continuity with the tradition out of which it emerged and adaptation to a new political context.

About the author

A. K. Shauku is an assistant professor of political science and public administration at State University of New York College at Buffalo. He primarily studies political and legal institutions.

Suggestions for further reading

In this book
See essays 8 (What Can States Do?), 13 (What Is the Purpose of the Separation of Powers?), 14 (The President as Chief Executive), and 26 (Term Lengths, Stability, and Responsiveness).

Elsewhere
Marbury v. Madison, 5 U.S. 137 (1803).

Thach, C. C. 1923. *The Creation of the Presidency, 1775–1789: A Study in Constitutional History*. Baltimore, MD: Johns Hopkins Press.

Declaration of the Immediate Causes Which Induce and Justify the Secession of South Carolina (1860). Available at https://avalon.law.yale.edu/ 19th_century/csa_scarsec.asp.

6

How Can We Tell What the Constitution Means?

Sara C. Benesh

How can we tell what the Constitution means? Well, we can read it. It's a relatively short document and can be found via a simple Google search. Still, if careful reading was all that was needed, we wouldn't have included this essay in this book—and you probably wouldn't be reading the book in the first place. Discerning the meaning of the Constitution can be very challenging for a number of reasons.

First, English is, in some respects, an imprecise language. Words sometimes have multiple definitions and sometimes can even simultaneously hold contradictory meanings. Imagine attempting to understand a sentence with the word *sanction* in it without any context as to whether it references a punishment or a reward.

Second, the Constitution is a set of compromises, some of which resulted in language that is (perhaps purposely) vague. What is "just compensation" required for a taking? What is "cruel and unusual punishment," forbidden by the Eighth Amendment? What exactly is an "unreasonable search," from which we are protected? And what in the world does "due process" include?

Third, the Constitution was written a very long time ago, before technology like cell phones or the internet was invented. Ascertaining what these old words mean to our time can be quite difficult. Does the freedom of the press mentioned in the First Amendment apply to an internet blogger? Do police need a search warrant to search a cell phone?

Because of these vague provisions, dated terms, and ambiguities, the justices of the Supreme Court must find a way to interpret the Constitution. They have, over time, used a variety of methods to do so.

Some justices, for example, follow the interpretive strategy of *textualism* or *plain meaning*, which argues for understanding the words exactly as they are written. Justice Black was a First Amendment textualist, maintaining that the First Amendment's admonition that "Congress shall make no law . . . abridging the freedom of speech" meant exactly that: *no law*. Any law that attempted to in some way regulate speech or the press (say on the grounds that it was obscene or libelous) was unconstitutional in his view. Perhaps it would surprise you to learn that while Justice Black saw the Constitution as precluding *any* legislation regulating speech, he was fine with banning students from wearing armbands in protest of the Vietnam War; they weren't actually speaking. While most of the justices interpreted the word "speech" to include actions akin to speech, Justice Black did not. Speech meant something different to him than it did to the majority in *Tinker v. Des Moines* (1969).

Other justices follow the interpretive strategy of *originalism* or *original meaning*, which seeks to understand what the words meant at the time they were written. An originalist justice would, for example, deem capital punishment to be wholly consistent with the Eighth Amendment, regardless of its method, without question, because, at the time the framers drafted the Eighth Amendment, capital punishment was routinely meted out, even for crimes that did not result in loss of life (including rape and arson, among others), often by public hanging (and sometimes worse). The words "cruel and unusual punishment," as understood by the framers then, surely would *not* apply to the death penalty as currently administered. Those justices who do not adhere to originalism, though, interpret those words differently and with reference to "evolving standards of decency that mark the progress of a maturing society" (*Trop v. Dulles*, 1958). Because more justices have agreed with that approach to interpreting the Eighth Amendment, the Court has collectively narrowed the crimes that can constitutionally be punished by death to whom the penalty can constitutionally be applied and by what method states may execute. These justices might be deemed *constitutional pragmatists*.

A justice who employs *pragmatism* as her guiding principle in understanding the meaning of the Constitution considers the words and the underlying concepts, evaluates various interpretations one could plausibly make of the text, and then balances the costs and benefits of employing one reading over another to come to the "best" resolution. A pragmatic reading of the Second Amendment, for example, might consider the societal impacts of deeming the provision to protect an individual right to bear arms rather than a collective, militia-based right. Pragmatism might also lead a justice to "find" a right in the Constitution, arguing that underlying principles and a balancing of consequences counsel in its favor. Privacy, for example, is a right established not by the text of the Constitution but rather by the justices' interpretation of terms like "due process" and the combination of provisions like the right to free assembly, protections against quartering soldiers, and the requirement that searches and seizures be reasonable. A textualist sees no right to privacy in the Constitution because it is not written down there. But do you have some notion that you have something called a right to privacy that ought to be considered pretty important?

The Constitution's meaning is not self-evident. All modes of constitutional interpretation (only a few of which were described here) have proponents and detractors. The result is that what the Constitution really means depends on the preferences and choices of those with the power to make authoritative interpretations, most importantly the justices of the Supreme Court.

About the author

Sara C. Benesh is an associate professor and chair of political science at the University of Wisconsin, Milwaukee. She studies judicial decision-making and institutional legitimacy.

Suggestions for further reading

In this book

See essays 7 (Is the Constitution What the Justices Say It Is?), 20 (Judicial Review), and 21 (The Challenge of Judicial Independence).

Elsewhere

Segal, Jeffrey A., and Harold J. Spaeth. 2012. *The Supreme Court and the Attitudinal Model Revisited*. New York: Cambridge University Press. Chap. 2.

Whittington, Keith E. 1999. *Constitutional Interpretation: Textual Meaning, Original Intent, and Judicial Review*. Lawrence: University Press of Kansas.

Rutkowski, Adam G. 2021. "Constitutional Interpretation Styles of US Supreme Court Justices." In *Open Judicial Politics*, 2nd ed., edited by Rorie Spill Solberg and Eric Waltenburg, 495–513. Corvallis: Oregon State University. https://open.oregonstate.education/open-judicial-politics/.

7
Is the Constitution What the Justices Say It Is?

Joseph L. Smith

The essays in this book attempt to explain the features of the Constitution. But in the current version of American politics, the Supreme Court is the primary interpreter of the Constitution. So is all this discussion of the Constitution's words and meaning naïve if the Supreme Court justices get to decide how it will apply?

Another way of asking this question is, "When the Supreme Court interprets the Constitution, is it the words of the Constitution or the justices' own policy views that determine their interpretations?" This is an important question because the rulings of the Court go a long way toward settling disagreements about what the Constitution means. To a great extent, the Constitution is what the justices say it is. But what they "say" may be constrained by the words of the Constitution and previous Court rulings.

Public opinion polls show that more than half of Americans believe Supreme Court justices are too influenced by their personal or political views. These Americans are not wrong. Justices nominated by Republican presidents vote systematically differently than justices nominated by Democrats. There are clear reasons why justices' political views might influence the way they interpret the Constitution.

First, the role of Supreme Court justice invites, or even requires, justices to use their own judgment. Many important parts of the Constitution are ambiguous. The phrases "due process of law" and "commerce among the several states" don't have obvious, definitive meanings. Applying these broad phrases to specific legal disputes leaves a lot of room for disagreement.

Another factor is the importance of the issues before the Court. The Constitution lays out fundamental borders of individual liberty and government authority. Justices are likely to have strong opinions that they cannot easily put aside while they are interpreting the document. In the current era, most justices have had long careers in public affairs before joining the Court, so they have settled ideas on important political issues. In fact, these preferences are one of the reasons they are selected to be justices.

Finally, justices are uniquely protected from the consequences of their job-related actions. They can't be fired, demoted, or have their pay docked for making bad decisions. The only way justices can be removed from their jobs is through impeachment, and no justice has ever been removed in this way. With no supervision, human nature leads them to follow their own viewpoint.

However, there are also factors that rein in the justices' freedom. For one thing, the words of the Constitution are available for anyone to see. Supreme Court decisions that ignore or misrepresent the text are likely to be called out by the press, politicians, and their fellow justices. This constraint works well for parts of the Constitution that are crystal clear, such as requirements that the president be at least thirty-five years old or the power of Congress to overturn a president's veto with a two-thirds majority.

A second factor that reduces justices' ability to play fast and loose with the Constitution is the tradition of writing opinions to justify their rulings. These opinions explain the reasoning behind their interpretations. These justifications can be discussed, dissected, and challenged. Justices who write or sign onto foolish opinions would be embarrassed.

Every Supreme Court case has lawyers for each side, each making the strongest arguments they can. They submit written arguments in advance and then respond to justices' questions during oral argument. This process ensures that the strongest arguments for each side are made. Justices who ignore significant arguments will look foolish.

Stare Decisis is a Latin term meaning "let the decision stand." It is also a norm within the judicial system meaning that justices should interpret laws and the Constitution so that they are consistent with previous decisions. It means justices should respect precedent. Every controversial part of the Constitution has been litigated scores of times, and so justices must either explain how their current interpretation is consistent with previous interpretations or explain why the previous interpretations were wrong.

The skeptical reader might wonder what mechanism enforces these norms that push justices to seriously consider precedent and the words of the Constitution. One answer is that like all of us, justices want the respect of their peers. In law school and as they are coming up through the legal profession, justices absorb the legal community's standards for good legal reasoning. The ability to reason like a lawyer is what distinguishes them from nonlawyers and makes them special. If their rulings aren't supported by good legal reasoning, they risk losing the esteem of fellow justices, lower court judges, the broader legal community, and even their own self-respect. The restraining effect of norms is reinforced by the need to get at least five justices to agree on any interpretation. To the extent that justices vote by ideology, this means getting the middle justice on the liberal-conservative spectrum to attach their reputation to the new interpretation. If the justices don't line up by ideology, it means getting five justices with different ideological perspectives to endorse the interpretation. This is part of the reason why the Court's interpretation of the Constitution usually changes slowly.

A final factor that keeps the Court from changing its interpretation of the Constitution every time it might be favored by a new majority of the Court is that the Court often needs the support of other branches to implement its decisions. Justices know this and so are unlikely to support new interpretations that are outside of the political mainstream.

The bottom line is that justices' personal views about good policy do influence how they read the Constitution, but there are also lots of reasons why they can't base their interpretations solely on their own preferences. How these different factors interact in any particular case is a complicated, and much-studied, question.

About the author

Joseph L. Smith is a professor and department chair in the Department of Political Science at the University of Alabama. His research focuses on decision-making in the United States federal courts.

Suggestions for further reading

In this book
See essays 6 (How Can We Tell What the Constitution Means?), 20 (Judicial Review), and 21 (The Challenge of Judicial Independence).

Elsewhere
Edelman, Paul H., David E. Klein, and Stefanie A. Lindquist. 2012. "Consensus, Disorder, and Ideology on the Supreme Court." *Journal of Empirical Legal Studies* 9 (1): 129–48.

Robinson, Rob. 2013. "Punctuated Equilibrium and the Supreme Court." *Policy Studies Journal* 41 (4): 654–81.

Congress and the States

8
What Can States Do?

John D. Nugent

Before the current Constitution was ratified in 1787, the young United States had been governed as a nation since 1781 by the Articles of Confederation. While that document outlined some areas where the national government would be dominant, it established only a weak "league of friendship" that left most governmental authority to the states, using national authority to oversee a few broad areas like national defense, diplomacy, and managing the westward expansion of the country. If we could have somehow bundled up states' legal authority and the national government's legal authority and put them on a scale in, say, 1784, the balance would have tilted heavily in the direction of the states.

The people who wrote the 1787 Constitution sought to shift this balance in the direction of the national government in order to fix problems and shortcomings that they perceived. They thought the country needed to become more *United* and less *States* if it was to pursue national goals like promoting economic development and conducting diplomacy and trade with other countries. And it needed a new way of collecting revenue to pay for its increased activity.

The enhanced powers of the new federal government were layered onto the existing arrangement of state governments, giving us a mixed "federalist" system in which multiple levels of government (national, local, and state) make laws and policies. While the national government in Washington has grown tremendously in size and scope since 1787, state governments still retain substantial powers to make decisions that affect our lives. This state authority is reflected in differences in tax rates, school funding, environmental controls, voting rules, and many other policies. The most important forms of state powers are known as the "police powers," which encompass the legal authority to pass laws to promote and protect the health, safety, and morals of their populations. In addition, states today have important roles in areas of business regulation, public education, taxation, and administering elections.

Through their power to protect health and safety, states are the first responders to problems such as opioid drug abuse, gun violence, suicide, and pandemics. Every state government has a department of public health that protects and promotes the health of its population by tracking health trends in the state; promoting immunization, vaccination, and other good practices; licensing health care and food-service facilities; identifying and responding to health hazards like asbestos and lead; and supporting education programs aimed at helping people make healthy choices (such as avoiding cigarette and drug use).

Similarly, all state governments have some form of a department of public safety that protects people by doing things such as collecting crime statistics; issuing driver's licenses; regulating firearms and promoting gun safety; inspecting and certifying the safety of facilities such as buildings, elevators, and amusement parks; operating a state police force; and responding to weather and other emergencies. State governments' responses to the COVID-19 pandemic have demonstrated the wide range of steps they can take (or decline to take) to protect public health and safety, often under the direction of governors exercising emergency powers.

People sometimes say that governments can't legislate morality, but since the beginnings of the nation, states have attempted to control behaviors that elected officials consider morally questionable. They continue to do so today through laws regulating the sale of alcohol and, increasingly, marijuana; licensing gambling and lotteries; restricting public nudity, pornography, and prostitution; establishing age limits for sexual consent and marriage; and determining whether and how to teach sex education in public schools.

In addition to these three areas of police powers, a fourth important area of state activity is the protection of property and regulation of business practices. Examples of this include state laws governing contracts, sales, leases, and lending. State governments also license a number of professions ranging from nurses to plumbers to barbers and hair stylists. State and local governments affect business and commercial development by regulating land use through zoning and other restrictions on property use. The vast majority of criminal law is created at the state level, under states' power to protect property and public safety.

A final area of state-governmental activity is the operation of public education systems—K–12 elementary and secondary schools as well as public community colleges and universities. Of the roughly 16.5 million students enrolled in two- or four-year colleges today, about 13 million are enrolled in public institutions run by states.

Through these powers, state governments affect large parts of everyday life. As long as they don't contradict valid federal law or the U.S. Constitution (which is ultimately controlling due to the supremacy clause), each of the fifty states has the independent authority to make its own laws in all of these areas, which can result in lots of variations from state to state. For example, during the COVID-19 pandemic, Illinois imposed strict limits on building occupancy and required masks even in outdoor spaces, while South Dakota imposed almost no restrictions.

Sometimes this variation is viewed negatively, as a "patchwork quilt" of laws that can be confusing or burdensome, and sometimes it is viewed positively, since it gives state officials the ability to respond to problems in their states in ways that are appropriate to local circumstances and consistent with the political views and political culture of the state's residents and leaders. You have probably heard people refer to "blue states" (where Democrats tend to control government) and "red states" (where Republicans typically prevail). States also vary in size (in population and square miles), the mix of industries and businesses there, and the state's ability and willingness to raise tax money to pay for government programs. All this variation means that it still matters in what state you live.

About the author

John D. Nugent is the director of institutional research and planning at Connecticut College in New London. His research has focused on how state officials influence federal policy-making.

Suggestions for further reading

In this book
See essays 6 (How Can We Tell What the Constitution Means?), 9 (What Is "Commerce among the Several States," and Why Does It Matter?), and 10 (What States Can't Do).

Elsewhere
Rozell, Mark J., and Clyde Wilcox. 2019. *Federalism: A Very Short Introduction*. New York: Oxford University Press.

Robertson, David Brian. 2017. *Federalism and the Making of America*, 2nd ed. New York: Routledge.

Governing. http://governing.com—A website with current news items on state and local government policy issues.

9

What Is "Commerce among the Several States," and Why Does It Matter?

H. W. Perry Jr.

> Congress shall have Power ... To regulate Commerce with foreign Nations, and among the several States, and with the Indian Tribes.
> —U.S. Constitution, Article I, Section 8

The commerce clause is the most important source of authority for the federal government's power to pass laws that govern us. The federal government is one of limited, enumerated powers and can only make laws that are "necessary and proper for carrying into execution" those powers. All other powers are left to the states (Tenth Amendment). Determining the boundary between federal and state domestic power has depended mostly on interpretations of the commerce clause. The broader the definition of commerce, the greater the scope of the national government's power to pass laws. As such, the extent of the commerce power has been, and remains, a source of constitutional dispute.

Under the Articles of Confederation, there was little ability to stop states from thwarting one another's commerce. Several provisions of the Constitution were designed to address this problem, but the most important eventually turned out to be the commerce clause, which gave the federal government the ability to regulate commerce "among the states" (now generally referred to as "interstate commerce"). The first major case involving the clause was *Gibbons v. Ogden* (1824). New York had granted a monopoly for operating steamboats in its waters. Chief Justice Marshall held the monopoly to be a violation of the commerce clause because a federal law licensing vessels in the coastal trade was deemed a regulation of commerce and therefore superseded New York's law. More importantly,

Marshall gave an expansive view of the scope of the clause offering definitions for the constitutional terms: "Commerce is . . . intercourse . . . and is regulated by prescribing rules for carrying on that intercourse."

The next major case did not arise until 1893, and it limited Marshall's broad definition. The Industrial Revolution was happening, as was the growth of national businesses and industries and an increasing concentration of economic power. According to the Court, a federal law that prohibited monopolies could not be extended to cover "monopolies in manufacture" because "commerce succeeds to manufacture and is not a part of it." Nonetheless, during the Progressive Era of the early 1900s, Congress passed laws to protect the health and safety of products and workers, but it did so indirectly by regulating their transportation. A 1914 case had upheld the federal government's regulation of *intra*state rail rates of *inter*state carriers because of their "close and substantial relation" to, and "substantial affect" upon, interstate traffic. With the Court's broadening of the understanding of what could be regulated under the commerce power, unsafe products or the products of child labor were banned from interstate commerce. The Supreme Court went along for a while, but these efforts came to a dramatic halt in *Hammer v. Dagenhart* (1918), when the Court gave a much narrower reading of the scope of interstate commerce. This pullback was happening in concert with the rise of laissez-faire ideology in some parts of society and on the Supreme Court. Not only did the Court strike down national efforts to regulate business as an invalid use of the commerce clause, but it also struck down state regulations for different constitutional reasons.

Then came the Great Depression, devastating the economy. There was a great clamor for action. FDR called for a "national solution to a national problem" and proposed his "New Deal." He was elected with huge Democratic majorities in Congress. Torrents of laws and actions from the federal government followed that forever changed the role of the national government. For a while, the Supreme Court struck down much of the New Deal legislation as being outside the authority to regulate interstate commerce. Then the famous Court packing plan was proposed, and though that failed, there was the "switch in time that saved nine," and the Court began upholding national regulations of the economy. Federal regulation of the economy continued to grow for decades. The commerce clause was even the source of the civil rights laws of 1964 that banned discrimination by private businesses—such as restaurants, hotels, theaters, and so on—based on race. The Fourteenth Amendment prohibited racial discrimination by governments, but for the most part, it did not reach the private sphere. The commerce clause is also the source of authority for regulating much crime at the national level. Since the New Deal, no laws have been struck down as an illegitimate use of the commerce clause so long as regulations are economic in nature and have a substantial effect on the economy. However, what is considered sufficiently economic in nature eventually became a source of debate.

The tide turned in *Lopez v. U.S.* (1995). The federal government as a regulation of commerce banned the possession of guns within a school zone. The Supreme Court struck down the law based on the commerce clause grounds. Soon after *Lopez*, the Court struck down portions of the "Violence against Women Act," despite demonstration by Congress that such violence has huge economic effects. In 2012, the Court held that the Affordable Care Act (Obamacare) was not a legitimate use of commerce clause authority (but the act was upheld under taxing authority). The Court did not disagree that Obamacare had huge economic effects but ruled that the activities being regulated were too many steps removed from commerce.

Despite the latest turn, the commerce clause will continue to be the principal constitutional authority for federal action, and most actions can be tied to the economy. Enhancing or restraining federal power will largely turn on politics rather than the Constitution, but the proper boundary of the commerce clause will remain a source of constitutional debate in politics and in constitutional law.

About the author

H. W. Perry Jr. is an associate professor of law, associate professor of government, and a University Distinguished Teaching Professor at the University of Texas at Austin. His research and teaching focus primarily on constitutional law and the U.S. Supreme Court.

Suggestions for further reading

In this book
See essays 6 (How Can We Tell What the Constitution Means?), 10 (What States Can't Do), and 45 (Regulating Private Discrimination).

Elsewhere
McCloskey, Robert G., and Sanford Levinson. 2016. *The American Supreme Court*. Chicago: University of Chicago Press.

United States v. Darby, 312 U.S. 100 (1941).

Wickard v. Filburn, 317 U.S. 111 (1942).

National Federation of Independent Business v. Sebelius, 567 U.S. 519 (2012).

10
What States Can't Do

Joseph L. Smith

This Constitution, and the laws of the United States which shall be made in pursuance thereof; and all treaties made, or which shall be made, under the authority of the United States, shall be the supreme Law of the Land; and the judges in every state shall be bound thereby, anything in the Constitution or laws of any State to the contrary notwithstanding.
—U.S. Constitution, Article VI, Section 2

Although states made most governing decisions when the Constitution was ratified, the scope of the national government's domain has dramatically increased over the last 230 years. This change stems primarily from the interaction among three constitutional provisions: the supremacy clause, Congress's enumerated powers, and the necessary and proper clause.

The Constitution's supremacy clause (art. VI, sec. 2) says that valid national laws, along with the Constitution and treaties, are the "supreme law of the land" and that, as supreme law, they supersede any state law. This begs the question, "What is a 'valid' national law?" The answer is in Article I, Section 8, which lays out the lawmaking powers of Congress. Any national law carrying out one of these powers is valid (provided it was passed using correct procedures).

Congress's powers in Article I, Section 8 are vast. They include the power to raise tax money to provide for the defense and "general welfare" of the country. Tradition and Supreme Court decisions have endorsed the view that Congress can spend money on anything it views as good for the country. This power has been the basis for constructing interstate highways, establishing national parks, and funding Medicaid and social security, among other things.

Congress can even use its spending power to push states to take actions favored by the national government. For example, when the national government wanted states to raise their drinking ages to twenty-one, it passed a law stipulating that states would lose 5 percent of their federal highway funds if they didn't comply. In response to South Dakota's lawsuit challenging the policy, the Supreme Court essentially endorsed use of money to buy state obedience. However, the Court did say that if the financial penalty for not complying was so severe that states could not realistically accept it, then the conditions on state aid might unconstitutionally infringe on state autonomy.

Beyond this broad spending power, Article I, Section 8 gives Congress the power to control immigration and citizenship, support the nation's armed forces, declare war, coin money, set up a postal service, and "regulate Commerce . . . among the several States." Early in our history, the Supreme Court defined this last power broadly, and it has become more important over time. The national economy has grown from a collection of isolated, primitive industries into a vast interconnected web. All significant commerce is now interstate commerce and as such can be regulated by the national government.

These enumerated powers are extensive, but they are further amplified by the necessary and proper clause at the end of Section 8. This part of the Constitution, sometimes called the elastic clause, allows Congress to make any law "necessary and proper" for carrying out the enumerated powers. In *McCulloch v. Maryland* (1819), the Supreme Court interpreted the clause to allow Congress to make any law that helps it carry out its enumerated powers, as long as the law doesn't violate another part of the Constitution.

For example, federal minimum wage, maximum hour, workplace safety, and environmental rules are not themselves regulations of interstate commerce, but they all help the national government achieve the goal of regulating interstate commerce, as do rules against discrimination in employment, housing, and business. Laws against mail fraud are extensions of the authority to set up a postal service. The bottom line is that the Constitution gives a lot of power to the national government.

Why can't states also make their own rules covering these areas granted to the national government? In some cases, they can. Like the national government, states can impose taxes, create court systems, and enforce criminal laws. Other areas are explicitly off-limits to states. Article I, Section 10 prohibits states from engaging in international agreements, coining money, collecting tariffs, and a few other things. Beyond this, it gets more complicated. State authority is limited by two concepts.

The first concept is *preemption*. In this context, *preemption* means that valid national laws can displace the state's right to legislate on the same subjects if national laws were intended to prohibit state regulation or if state policy would conflict or interfere with the operation of the national laws. Whether a national law preempts state control depends on the details of the national law. For example, in *Arizona v. U.S.* (2012), the Court held that a series of national laws specifying the rights and duties of noncitizens in the U.S. meant that states could not add their own requirements or enforcement mechanisms. Conversely, the Court has held that Oregon's Death with Dignity Act, which allows physicians to prescribe drugs with which a terminally ill person can end their life, was not preempted by the national government's Controlled Substances Act.

The second concept goes by the funny name of *dormant commerce clause*. This doctrine, created by the Supreme Court in 1851, means that there are some aspects of interstate commerce that states are barred from regulating, even if the national government has not passed any laws on the subject. States are generally not allowed to do anything that restricts interstate transportation, even if states argue these limits are necessary to keep their residents safe. For example, an Arizona law limiting the lengths of trains was declared unconstitutional because it interfered too much with interstate transportation.

The Constitution gives the national government control over a very wide swath of human activity and provides that valid national laws trump state laws. The integration of the national economy and long-standing Supreme Court doctrine has simultaneously expanded the scope of national authority and placed substantial limits on what states can control.

About the author

Joseph L. Smith is a professor and department chair in the Department of Political Science at the University of Alabama. His research focuses on decision-making in the United States federal courts.

Suggestions for further reading

In this book
See essays 8 (What Can States Do?), 9 (What Is "Commerce among the Several States," and Why Does It Matter?), and 40 (How Did the Civil War Amendments Change the Constitution?).

Elsewhere
McCulloch v. Maryland, 17 U.S. 316 (1819).

Southern Pacific Company v. Arizona, 325 U.S. 761 (1945).

11

How Can Governments Use the Power to Tax?

Jolly A. Emrey

It should come as no surprise that the power to tax was one of the issues most debated by the framers of the Constitution. Although they recognized that taxation is a necessary tool for government to raise revenue, they also understood that it has the potential to be used as a blunt instrument. Our federalist system, with national and state concurrent powers to tax, can make it all the more complicated. As Chief Justice John Marshall wrote in *McCulloch v. Maryland* (1819), a case that involved the state of Maryland seeking to tax the national government, "The power to tax involves the power to destroy." The Supreme Court wisely ruled that states do not have the power to tax the national government. One can imagine how quickly the United States national government would have ceased to exist if the ruling had been in favor of the state of Maryland.

Both the positive and negative aspects of taxation's power can be seen in "sin taxes." If you smoke tobacco products or you drink alcohol, chances are you pay a state tax to do so. A twenty-first-century example of this is the recreational use of marijuana where states have dispensaries and regulate its production and sales. Through sin taxes, states believe that they can curb undesirable behavior by adding cost to products. People will consume less, theoretically, because the tax adds to the cost of consumption. Sin taxes are also applied to gasoline in most states to encourage people to drive less and collectively reduce carbon emissions. Taxes on gambling winnings, including lotteries, are another example of taxation as regulation.

Successful sin taxes not only modify behavior; they also generate more state revenue. For many states, the annual revenue from sin taxes ranges from hundreds of millions of dollars to over one billion. Of course, there is a paradox here: states are actually relying on people to engage in "sinful" behavior in order to capture these sizable revenues. Marijuana is an excellent example of states recognizing a revenue opportunity and shifting from criminalizing a behavior to regulating it in a profitable way. The state of Oregon was able to collect over one billion dollars in 2020 from marijuana sales alone.

What are the limits on the power to tax? Most importantly, neither the national government nor state governments may create or enforce taxation schemes that infringe on individuals' constitutional rights. Each level of government also has some special limitations.

States' taxing power may not be used in a way that conflicts with a constitutional power of the national government. It is unconstitutional for state governments to tax on the basis of an individual's residency in a different state. And states may not create taxes that protect their own economies or place burdens on trade among the states. Taxes such as these would have the effect of not only protecting economies within states but also hurting the economies of other states and, perhaps, the national economy as a whole. In essence, those kinds of taxes place a burden on interstate commerce.

National taxes must be uniform. Congress is specifically required by Article I, Section 8 of the Constitution to treat all states the same when it enacts a tax. The framers understood well that the power to tax could be used as a weapon against some states, or regions of states, if the national government wasn't specifically constrained.

A novel constitutional question that the Supreme Court of the United States was recently asked to review was whether or not a tax of zero dollars is actually a tax. This issue involved a challenge to the United States Affordable Care Act (ACA), which was adopted in 2010. The ACA's validity had been challenged in the Supreme Court previously. In 2012, it was argued that the U.S. Congress did not have the constitutional authority to create the ACA in *National Federation of Independent Business v. Sebelius*. The Supreme Court ruled that the ACA was valid legislation because of the national government's *power to tax*. The ACA included a tax set at $695 that only applied if adults did not have health insurance. In 2016, Congress reduced the ACA's tax from $695 to $0. In reaction, Texas and several other states filed suit. They argued, among other things, that without an actual dollar amount, the tax became nothing more than a "toothless" mandate that was not tied to a specific constitutional power. Simply put, a tax of $0 was not a tax. And if there was no tax in the ACA, the creation of the ACA was an invalid exercise of congressional power.

When the Supreme Court ruled on this case (*California v. Texas*) in June 2021, it did not actually address the tax question. Instead, the justices focused on an important technical issue of standing to sue and determined that the states did not have the right to have their case heard because they could not demonstrate how the revision inflicted injury or harm.

So whether or not a tax of $0 is still a tax is an unresolved puzzle that is interesting to consider and may be addressed by the Supreme Court of the United States in a future term. What we can be sure of is that governments at all levels will continue to find creative ways to exercise the power to tax.

About the author

Jolly A. Emrey is an associate professor of political science and department chair at the University of Wisconsin-Whitewater. She works primarily on state courts in the United States and courts in Ireland.

Suggestions for further reading

In this book
See essays 8 (What Can States Do?), 9 (What Is "Commerce among the Several States," and Why Does It Matter?), and 10 (What States Can't Do).

Elsewhere
McCulloch v. Maryland, 17 U.S. 316 (1819).

Nat. Fedn. of Indep. Business v. Sebelius, 567 U.S. 519 (2012).

12
Why Is It Hard to Sue a State?

Susan W. Johnson

Imagine you work for a state corrections system, and your employer requires you to work overtime without extra pay. According to federal law, your employer is responsible for paying you extra if you work more than forty hours per week. Can you sue the state for its failure to comply? Most people would probably assume yes. However, as some Maine probation officers learned in 1999, it's not so simple. When they tried to sue Maine for violating the Fair Labor Standards Act, the U.S. Supreme Court ruled in *Alden v. Maine* that the suit could not go forward; it was prevented by state sovereign immunity. The doctrine of sovereign immunity dates back to the common law of England, where it provides that the Crown as sovereign is free from the law's provisions and not subject to suits in the courts it creates. While not explicitly mentioning it in the U.S. Constitution, the founders generally accepted this conception of sovereignty, considering it fundamental to statehood. However, while its application to the federal government has been fairly uncontroversial, deciding what sovereignty means for the states of the union has been much more complicated.

States have special standing in the U.S. system because the Constitution rejected a system where power is centralized solely in a national government. However, it also rejected a confederation of coequal, independent sovereign states. After all, the Articles of Confederation failed largely because they provided too much power to the states and not enough to the federal government. The Constitution tried to strike a balance. It established supremacy of national authority, with important limitations on states, but also embraced some aspects of state independence.

This ambiguity in the extent of state power, dating back to the founding, provides competing frameworks in the interpretation of sovereignty and immunity from lawsuits. Is the Constitution a contract between the federal government and the states who ratified it? In this line of reasoning, federal power was carved from existing powers passed from the Crown to the states at America's founding; therefore, states are sovereign entities with broad protection from lawsuits just as the sovereign Crown enjoyed. Or is the Constitution a contract directly between the federal government and the people? Viewed in this framework, states—unlike the federal government—are not entitled to broad immunity from suit.

One provision of the Constitution, the Eleventh Amendment, embraces an aspect of state sovereign immunity. The Eleventh Amendment bars citizens from suing another state directly in federal court, a reaction to a lawsuit pursued against Georgia by two South Carolinians in 1793 to collect a Revolutionary War debt. In *Chisholm v. Georgia* (1793), the U.S. Supreme Court allowed the citizen suit against the state. However, the ruling was controversial, and the states and Congress quickly ratified the Eleventh Amendment, barring such citizen suits in federal courts, one of only a handful of times the Court has been overruled by a constitutional amendment. States insisted they were sovereign and that immunity from suit was an essential aspect of their sovereignty, as they had been assured of by Alexander Hamilton in his defense of the Constitution to the states for ratification.

Although state sovereign immunity wasn't an especially pressing constitutional issue for many years, it has risen to prominence again in recent decades. In 1996, the U.S. Supreme Court embraced an expansive view of state sovereign immunity in *Seminole Tribe of Florida v. Florida*. The Seminole Tribe filed suit against Florida under a federal law that allowed tribal suits against states in federal court. However, the Court ruled that the Eleventh Amendment prevents Congress from authorizing suits against states in federal court even by citizens of the state being sued.

When the Supreme Court handed down its ruling in *Seminole Tribe*, the probation officers' case against Maine was pending in a lower federal court. Since the federal suit was barred, the probation officers were then forced to turn to state court as the venue for suing Maine. In ruling against them in *Alden v. Maine*, the Court held that sovereign immunity also protects states from being sued in their own state courts. Writing for the majority, Justice Kennedy reasoned that immunity from suits in their own courts existed for states at ratification and is protected by the Tenth Amendment as a reserved state power.

Thus, states may be required to follow certain labor or other types of federal regulations, but enforcement is limited, and recourse may not be available through lawsuits against the state. State sovereign immunity advocates argue it is necessary for guarding against lawsuits that would potentially bankrupt a state and that it protects state interests against federal overreach. Opponents, including Justice Souter, who dissented in both *Seminole Tribe* and *Alden v. Maine*, maintain that in the U.S. constitutional system, sovereignty rests not with the states but with the people and that suits against states should be broadly authorized.

About the author

Susan W. Johnson is a professor of political science at the University of North Carolina at Greensboro. Her research interests include judicial politics, comparative courts, and gender.

Suggestions for further reading

In this book
See essays 8 (What Can States Do?) and 40 (How Did the Civil War Amendments Change the Constitution?).

Elsewhere
The Federalist Papers no. 81.

Seminole Tribe of Florida v. Florida, 517 U.S. 44 (1996).

Alden v. Maine, 527 U.S. 706 (1999).

Conflicts between the Branches

13
What Is the Purpose of the Separation of Powers?

Joseph L. Smith

> The accumulation of all powers, legislative, executive, and judiciary, in the same hands, whether of one, a few, or many, and whether hereditary, self-appointed, or elective, may justly be pronounced the very definition of tyranny.
>
> —*The Federalist Papers* no. 47

These words, from James Madison's *Federalist Paper* 47, set out the goals of the Constitution's separation of powers: to preserve liberty by dividing power and giving each branch the incentives and tools to protect its powers. The framers of the Constitution separated the functions of governing into three categories: making laws (the legislative power), enforcing laws (the executive power), and authoritatively settling disputes about the law (the judicial power). To the framers, history showed that whenever any unified group gained full control of these three functions, that group would end up invading the liberty of the people they ruled. Even if they believe they are acting for the common good, rulers love power and are unlikely to restrain themselves.

One of the main strategies for protecting liberty was to fragment government power. The first words in Articles I, II, and III separate these powers by giving the legislative, executive, and judicial powers, respectively, to Congress, the president, and the Supreme Court. The framers assumed that political officials would want to increase their own power and influence. By separating these functions into different branches, the framers hoped that the officials exercising each function would try to preserve and increase the powers of their own branch. The competition for power among the branches would keep each in check. In addition, the officials in each branch are selected in different ways, meaning that they will have different backgrounds and different constituencies to please. This should help them see political issues from different angles and decrease the likelihood that they work together to invade liberty.

Because politicians seek to expand their powers, telling each branch to stick to its own function would likely not be enough. In addition to giving each branch its own function and the incentive to protect its powers, the Constitution gives to each branch the tools to protect its turf. These are the "checks and balances": powers that allow each branch to play a role in the other branches' business. The president can veto legislation passed by Congress and choose nominees for the federal courts. Congress has the power to impeach the president and can reject treaties and nominations proposed by the president. Congress has the power to create federal courts in addition to the Supreme Court and regulate their jurisdictions. The Supreme Court can review laws and actions taken by the other two branches and can decline to apply those determined to be unconstitutional. Given these overlapping powers, a more accurate description of the separation of powers is "separate institutions sharing powers."

But there is disagreement about the extent of the powers each branch can rightfully wield. This system, which starts by assigning different functions to different branches but then gives each branch a role in the other branches' functions, is destined to generate arguments about the exact scope of legislative, executive, and judicial powers and about how much one branch can interfere in the others' business.

For example, the president is commander in chief of the military, but Congress is given the power to declare war. This gives rise to the question of whether and how the president can use the U.S. military to advance or protect U.S. interests without Congress's consent. Currently, presidents often act without Congress's consent in carrying out military missions, even when that means inserting troops into hostile situations.

The Supreme Court reviews federal laws and actions to determine if they are constitutional, but Article III, Section 2 gives Congress the right to remove cases or topics from the Court's appellate jurisdiction. So can Congress evade judicial review by removing a topic from the Court's jurisdiction? In an 1869 case, the Court meekly abandoned its review of a case, even though it had already held arguments.

Congress frequently disagrees with the president about how federal statutes should be enforced. This sort of disagreement is almost unavoidable because so many statutes delegate broad policy-making powers to the executive branch. Congress developed a tool called a "legislative veto" to maintain some control over how a law is implemented. A legislative veto allows Congress to disapprove selected policy actions by executive branch officials carrying out the law. In a 1983 case, the Supreme Court declared the legislative veto unconstitutional on the grounds that Congress was trying to control the law without going through the lawmaking process outlined in the Constitution.

Congress and the president have also squared off over investigations of illegal conduct in the executive branch. Investigating crimes is traditionally an executive function, but if the executive branch controls all investigations, who will investigate possible crimes in the executive branch? In 1987, the Supreme Court upheld Congress's right to set up a process that allowed such investigations to be conducted outside the president's control.

The Supreme Court has historically taken one of two approaches to disputes over the separation of powers. The "formalist" approach emphasizes strict definitions of executive, legislative, and judicial powers and keeps each branch in its own lane. The 1983 decision declaring legislative vetoes unconstitutional is an example of a formalist approach.

The "functionalist" approach, on the other hand, is more pragmatic and flexible, taking into account the realities of the political system and allowing some relaxation of a strict separation of powers. The 1987 decision exemplifies this pragmatic approach, because it allowed Congress to set rules about a core function of the executive branch, investigating crimes. One way of thinking about these two approaches is that formalism emphasizes separation of powers while functionalism prioritizes checks and balances.

The separation of powers system was designed to make it harder for the government to abuse the governed. Complicated though it is to understand and implement, it probably accomplishes its main goal.

About the author

Joseph L. Smith is a professor and department chair in the Department of Political Science at the University of Alabama. His research focuses on decision-making in the United States federal courts.

Suggestions for further reading

In this book

See essays 16 (Who Really Makes the Laws?), 18 (Can the President Start a War?), 20 (Judicial Review), and 21 (The Challenge of Judicial Independence).

Elsewhere

The Federalist Papers nos. 47, 48, and 51.

Youngstown Sheet & Tube Co. v. Sawyer, 343 U.S. 579 (1952).

14

The President as Chief Executive

David Crockett

When people think of chief executives, they tend to think of people like Bill Gates or Jeff Bezos—powerful individuals who run their own companies, making decisions that shape the nature of commercial activity around the globe. But is that the template we should use when thinking about the president of the United States? It doesn't take a lot of work comparing Franklin Roosevelt to Calvin Coolidge, or Ronald Reagan to Gerald Ford, to recognize that models of executive leadership in the American presidency are pretty diverse.

Even given that diversity of experience, however, all presidents occupy the same constitutional space as chief executive. They all swear an oath to "preserve, protect, and defend the Constitution of the United States," and they are all charged by the Constitution to "take care that the laws be faithfully executed." Alexander Hamilton stated the duty of the president most succinctly in *Federalist* no. 75, arguing that the function of the "executive magistrate" was "the execution of the laws and the employment of the common strength."

From one perspective, then, all presidents do what chief executives in the commercial sector do. They set an agenda, typically through such constitutional mechanisms as the State of the Union address and the power to recommend legislation. They serve as crisis managers—national security crises, economic crises, or natural disasters—seen most obviously in the president's role as commander in chief. And they execute the laws of the land. Roosevelt or Coolidge, Reagan or Ford—each of them performed these functions.

One way to understand the president's potential power as chief executive is to compare the opening phrases of Articles I and II of the Constitution. Article I states, "All legislative Powers herein granted shall be vested in a Congress of the United States." The powers "herein granted" are found in Section 8, which gives us a specific laundry list of congressional powers. Article II, however, reads simply, "The executive

Power shall be vested in a President of the United States of America"—no qualification or constraint.

How should we interpret this difference in phrasing? Interestingly enough, both James Madison and Alexander Hamilton confronted this question in different circumstances during George Washington's presidency. Both argued that this vesting clause includes all executive powers, except where legislative participation is explicitly called for. In other words, the president possesses "the executive power," and that power should be understood broadly to include *all* traditional executive functions, except where the Constitution explicitly states otherwise—things like declaring war, ratifying treaties, and staffing key executive branch and judicial branch positions. After all, if we're going to hold the president responsible for preserving, protecting, and defending the Constitution and for taking care that the laws are faithfully executed, he has to have significant authority over "the executive power."

Historically, presidents have not agreed even among themselves on how to operationalize presidential power. Theodore Roosevelt and William Howard Taft, for example, famously disagreed with each other over how presidents should make use of their powers. These two men had once been close friends, but differences of opinion over how the chief executive should run the presidency drove them apart and made them enemies.

After his failed run for a third term in 1912, Roosevelt wrote his autobiography, in which he explained his approach to the presidency. Roosevelt saw the president as a "steward of the people," with the right and duty "to do anything that the needs of the nation demanded unless such action was forbidden by the Constitution or by the laws." He claimed he "acted for the public welfare," doing whatever was necessary "unless prevented by direct constitutional or legislative prohibition." In other words, the president can do whatever is necessary for the public interest, unless either the Constitution or congressional statute explicitly forbids it.

Following his term in office, Taft wrote a book about the presidency, directly attacking Roosevelt's expansive view of executive power. Taft believed Roosevelt's position was an "unsafe doctrine" that could lead to unlimited power. Instead, Taft argued that "the President can exercise no power which cannot be fairly and reasonably traced to some specific grant of power," and that power "must be either in the Federal Constitution or in an act of Congress passed in pursuance thereof." In other words, the president must connect his actions to a specific source of authority, constitutional or statutory. He can't just do something because he thinks it's in the public interest.

While these two approaches help explain the different ways some presidents have operated in American history, it is safe to say that over the past one hundred years, executive power has leaned in Roosevelt's direction. This is primarily because of what Roosevelt's cousin, Franklin Roosevelt, accomplished during the New Deal. The management challenge posed by the greatest economic crisis in American history prompted Congress to pass the Reorganization Act of 1939, allowing FDR to create the Executive Office of the President. So where Abraham Lincoln prosecuted the Civil War with only 2 assistants, FDR had 45 by the end of World War II. In 2021, the White House Office listed 560 personnel.

Presidents today have many hundreds of people working directly for them, giving them tremendous resources to craft a policy agenda, respond to crises, and execute the law. How presidents make use of these resources and whether they lead to greater success, either for the president or the nation, remain items of significant scholarly inquiry.

About the author

David Crockett is a professor of political science at Trinity University in San Antonio, Texas. His primary area of research is the American presidency and presidential elections.

Suggestions for further reading

In this book
See essays 15 (The Crucial Power to Appoint and Remove Officials), 16 (Who Really Makes the Laws?), 17 (Executive Orders: Statutes in Disguise?), 18 (Can the President Start a War?), and 19 (How Can We Get Rid of a Bad President?).

Elsewhere
The Federalist Papers no. 75.

Roosevelt, Theodore. 1913. *An Autobiography*. New York: Macmillan.

Tulis, Jeffrey K. 1987. *The Rhetorical Presidency*. Princeton, NJ: Princeton University Press.

15
The Crucial Power to Appoint and Remove Officials

Robert J. Hume

The power to appoint and remove government officials is one of the central constitutional issues associated with the president's ability to execute the laws. How much power do presidents have to hire, and fire, the people in government who are responsible for the day-to-day administration of the laws? The reason the question is so important is that presidents cannot govern effectively if they cannot manage the people who help them execute the laws. The federal government is far too big for presidents to manage alone, so today we have a vast federal bureaucracy composed of cabinet departments and other federal agencies.

Federal bureaucrats are not elected, and in theory, they advance the president's agenda. But whether the bureaucracy actually does act in tandem with the president depends, in part, on how much control the president has over their removal. When presidents have the removal power, they have more control over whether the administration of the laws is occurring consistently with their wishes. Presidential control over the bureaucracy can be beneficial because it ensures that the administration of government reflects what the people elected their president to do. However, too much presidential control risks presidential interference with areas of policy they do not understand and may tempt presidents to manipulate policy for their party's benefit.

Among the reasons the control of the bureaucracy is contested is that the Constitution says nothing about it. Article II, Section 2 states that presidents shall make appointments to federal offices "by and with the Advice and Consent of the Senate" but is silent about the process for removal. The main question is whether the Senate, which votes to confirm appointments, is also supposed to play a role in their removal. At various times in our history, the Senate has insisted that it is, even when it comes to the president's cabinet.

Perhaps the most famous of these occasions was the passage of the Tenure of Office Act of 1867. Congress enacted this law after the Civil War, during Reconstruction, to prevent President Andrew Johnson from replacing his cabinet officers with appointees who would be more lenient to the former confederate states. The act prohibited presidents from removing federal officers without Senate approval. President Johnson thought the act was unconstitutional, so he decided to test its constitutionality by firing his secretary of war, Edwin Stanton. Congress responded by impeaching Johnson.

After the Johnson impeachment, Congress assumed it had the removal power, so it attached provisions barring presidential removal to numerous federal offices. However, their constitutional status was uncertain. One of these offices was the position of postmaster, which became the center of the landmark case *Myers v. United States* (1926). The *Myers* opinion was written by Chief Justice William Howard Taft, who himself had been a president. Perhaps not surprisingly, Taft was sympathetic to the president's power to remove and wrote a broad opinion in *Myers* suggesting that the removal power was the president's alone. While Taft conceded that Article II, Section 2 was silent about removal, he thought other parts of the Constitution implied the power. Article II, Section 1 vested the "executive power" in the president, and Section 3 charged presidents to "take care that the laws be faithfully executed." Taft thought these provisions, read together, pointed toward presidents having the removal power and that Congress could not impose limits on it.

The problem was that Chief Justice Taft underestimated the scope of the federal bureaucracy and the types of federal agencies that existed or would be necessary. While some federal agencies are located within the executive branch and can be thought of as extensions of the president's prerogative to "take care the laws be faithfully executed," others are better understood as extensions of Congress. Just as presidents cannot do their jobs alone, Congress also needs help, so it delegates rule-making responsibility to independent agencies staffed by experts in specialized areas of policy, such as civil rights, consumer product safety, and trade.

In a subsequent case, *Humphrey's Executor v. United States* (1935), the Supreme Court clarified that Congress can make the heads of independent agencies immune from presidential removal when they perform "quasi-legislative" and "quasi-judicial" functions. The logic was that some areas of policy are so specialized that you need experts, not politicians, at the helm. These agencies are meant to be independent of politics and so must be safe from the threat of presidential removal. For example, the Federal Trade Commission, which was the subject of *Humphrey's Executor*, is headed by five commissioners who serve seven-year terms, with no more than three commissioners from the same political party.

In reality, the differences among executive, legislative, and judicial functions can be difficult to parse, making it hard to know which types of officials should be subject to removal. For example, *Seila Law v. Consumer Financial Protection Bureau* (2020) focused on the Consumer Financial Protection Bureau (CFPB), an independent agency responsible for consumer protection in the financial sector. Its structure differed from other independent agencies: the CFPB has broad enforcement powers that are executive in character, but unlike other independent agencies, it is headed by a single director instead of a multimember board. A narrow majority in *Seila Law* decided these differences mattered, and the director must be removable by the president.

More importantly, the Court signaled that it was more sympathetic to *Myers* than *Humphrey's Executor* and a return to a more robust understanding of the president's removal power. A strengthened removal power promises to give presidents more control over the bureaucracy, but it may come at the cost of making it harder for public officials to resist political influence and make policy in the national interest. The Court will need to consider how to strike the right balance between political oversight and professional administration of government.

About the author

Robert J. Hume is a professor of political science at Fordham University. He focuses on law and policy.

Suggestions for further reading

In this book
See essays 14 (The President as Chief Executive) and 29 (Is the Administrative State Unconstitutional?).

Elsewhere
Humphrey's Executor v. United States, 295 U.S. 602 (1935).

Seila Law v. Consumer Financial Protection Bureau, 140 S. Ct. 2183 (2020).

16

Who Really Makes the Laws?

Eric Heberlig

Congress makes the law, as anyone who has watched Schoolhouse Rock's "I'm Just a Bill" knows. Well, it's not quite that simple. As the legislative branch in our constitutional system, Congress has an advantage in lawmaking in most areas of domestic policy. Yet that advantage doesn't keep presidents from tussling for influence and often getting their way, particularly when it comes to budgets and foreign policy.

Congress is generally seen as slow, conflictual, and chaotic. Nevertheless, every session, it passes legislation addressing numerous serious public policy problems. Congress is organized to winnow down many ideas— some promising, others half-baked—into those that have the greatest likelihood of achieving their intended social goals while simultaneously having broad political support. One reason why Congress is slow and con-flictual is that it is representative. Legislators take seriously their responsibility to advocate the diverse perspectives of their constituents in their states and districts. The public policy results are thus often compromises that spread benefits widely across many groups and minimize visible costs.

Presidents bring lots of media attention to their proposals through their election campaigns, State of the Union addresses, and calls to the public to support their ideas. Presidents use their ability to capture public attention to pressure Congress to prioritize the president's issues. When presidents dramatize an issue, Congress is more likely to take action. When Congress does so, however, its members often substitute their vision of good public policy for the president's or pass a compromise rather than just approving what the president wants. Furthermore, most bills that Congress considers do not draw presidential attention. On most issues, Congress has considerable latitude to make policies based on what a majority in the House and the Senate can agree upon.

Congress's responses to presidential proposals largely depend on whether the president's party holds unified control of Congress or there is a divided party government, where the opposition party controls one or more chambers of Congress. Presidents have higher legislative success scores under a unified party government. It's easier to be persuasive when majorities in Congress already agree with your ideas! A Congress controlled by the opposition party may pass legislation, but often that legislation is more detailed, so as to keep the executive branch from implementing the law in ways that are inconsistent with the preferences of the congressional majority. Presidents' popularity plays a smaller role than their party's legislative majorities in their legislative success. As the political parties have polarized ideologically over time, the partisan alignment between the president and Congress has become even more important. The default position of members of the president's party is to support his agenda, and the other party's default position is to oppose it. In fact, vote analyses find that the parties in Congress polarize on votes when the president takes a position on a bill, even when the bill has no ideological content. And members of Congress sometimes switch their positions on issues, such as raising the debt ceiling, when the president of their party is in power. Members of Congress have an incentive to make sure their team looks competent.

Congress's shift toward passing fewer but larger "omnibus" bills also increases presidential leverage. Large, complex, "must-pass" bills that involve multiple policy areas are going to involve negotiation with the president. The president can use his veto power as leverage to bargain with congressional leaders to assure that his key policy priorities are met in the legislation.

The two areas where presidents exert the most influence over Congress are the budget and foreign policy. Though Congress has constitutional authority over taxing and spending, it has delegated the power to propose the budget to the president since the 1920s. As a consequence, Congress largely reacts to the president's budget and usually makes only marginal changes. While budgets may seem boring and like they're "just numbers," they are the government's most important policy decisions, because the government can't do anything unless someone is paid to implement the law. Moreover, budgets are statements of our value priorities—spending money on something says it's important and we want more of it. Thus, budgetary proposal power allows the president to set our priorities. Recent budget disputes between the president and Congress under a divided party government show how seriously both parties take the power over the budget. Budgets have taken longer to resolve with both sides playing a "game of chicken" trying to force the other side to give in before a government shutdown or to take the blame for the shutdown.

The second area of presidential domination is foreign and national security policy. Particularly in a crisis, presidents' invocations of their "commander in chief" title, ability to make decisions quickly, access to intelligence information and other diplomatic secrets, and ability to cite precedents of previous presidents give them the ability to deploy troops into hostile situations without congressional authorization. Presidents' abilities to negotiate treaties, appoint and receive ambassadors, and act as the spokesperson for the United States gives them influence over foreign policy generally. Despite having specific constitutional foreign policy powers, including the power to declare war, Congress often sees good policy reasons for the president to take the lead and not much political payoff in intervening. Congress can support the troops when things are going well and criticize the president's decisions when they aren't. The fact that Congress passed the War Powers Act to regain some of its national security power after the Vietnam War but has been consistently unable to follow through in holding the president accountable demonstrates Congress's institutional and political limitations in foreign and national security policy.

It is fair to conclude that policy-making in domestic policy is generally collaborative—if rough and tumble—with balanced influence between Congress and the president in most areas of public policy. In foreign policy, however, there is clear presidential dominance due to the president's natural advantages and deference by Congress.

About the author

Eric Heberlig is a professor of political science and public administration at the University of North Carolina Charlotte. He researches the politics of Congress, interest groups, elections, and campaign finance.

Suggestions for further reading

In this book
See essays 17 (Executive Orders: Statutes in Disguise?) and 29 (Is the Administrative State Unconstitutional?).

Elsewhere
Lee, Frances. 2009. *Beyond Ideology*. Chicago: University of Chicago Press.

Peterson, Mark A. 1993. *Legislating Together*. Cambridge, MA: Harvard University Press.

Sinclair, Barbara. 2016. *Unorthodox Lawmaking*. Washington: CQ Press.

17
Executive Orders: Statutes in Disguise?

Chris Edelson

The constitutional system contains a paradox when it comes to presidential power. The president is subject to the rule of law, operates within a constitutional framework that includes three branches of national government, and cannot simply do as he or she pleases. However, every president has found ways to take unilateral actions advancing their policy goals without going through the ordinary legislative process. The Supreme Court has concluded that unilateral presidential action can sometimes be justified and have the force of law, which means presidents can effectively make law without Congress's specific approval.

How can presidents take unilateral action to transform policy objectives into law when the Constitution states that "All legislative Powers herein granted shall be vested in a Congress of the United States"? Isn't this a violation of the separation of powers?

Making sense of these questions depends on understanding the history of executive orders, executive agreements, and other unilateral presidential actions and also understanding what the separation of powers means in the context of the Constitution. Madison explained in *The Federalist Papers* that the separation of powers is intended not to hermetically seal each branch of government in its own insular box but instead to ensure that no one branch accumulates excessive power. In Madison's view, this goal could only be accomplished if there is overlap between the different branches of government. For instance, while members of Congress pass legislation, the president can veto it. While the president is commander in chief of the military, it is left to Congress to declare war. Congress may vote for legislation that the president signs into law, but federal courts can use judicial review to strike it down, exercising an implied power not expressly written into the Constitution.

The separation of powers was designed to achieve two competing goals: providing the federal government with enough power to address national problems while also setting limits on power and preventing the rise of tyranny. The framers of the Constitution did not intend to create a new monarch but understood there would be times when presidents must act alone, without specific authorization from Congress. Presidents since Washington have exercised implied power to take unilateral action—although, following the Madisonian understanding of the separation of powers, such action can (at least in theory) be reined in by the other branches of government or by voters in elections. Presidential actions can alternatively receive approval after they are taken—for instance, Lincoln's Emancipation Proclamation was later endorsed and expanded by the Thirteenth Amendment. While presidents can take unilateral action, they don't necessarily have the last word.

Executive orders are the most well-known way in which presidents can take unilateral action. When properly supported by legal authority flowing from either the Constitution or federal statute, executive orders have the force of law. Executive orders give directions to executive branch officials but can have an impact beyond the executive branch. More than fourteen thousand executive orders have been issued since 1789, although the precise number is unknown because records were not kept until the twentieth century. The use of executive orders dramatically increased with Theodore Roosevelt, reaching a high-water mark with Franklin D. Roosevelt. Executive orders and other unilateral presidential actions can address relatively trivial matters as well as momentous initiatives. Some are seen as dangerous abuses of power, while others are viewed as historically transformative advances. For instance, FDR infamously issued Executive Order 9066 in February 1942, providing the U.S. military authority that it used to remove more than 110,000 Japanese Americans from their homes on the West Coast and confine them in internment camps during World War II. Six years later, Truman used Executive Order 9981 to end racial segregation in the military, an action now widely celebrated.

In addition to executive orders, there are more than twenty other mechanisms presidents have used to take unilateral action, including proclamations, memoranda, national security directives, and military orders. While statutory law requires most executive orders and proclamations to be made public, some unilateral actions can be kept secret, making it difficult to ensure accountability for abuses of power.

When executive orders and other presidential actions are publicly disclosed, there is a well-recognized framework that can be applied to determine their legitimacy. In *Youngstown Sheet & Tube Co. v. Sawyer*

(1952), the Supreme Court struck down an executive order Truman issued to authorize the seizure of steel factories in the United States. Justice Robert H. Jackson's concurring opinion described a three-part framework that is often used to evaluate presidential action; for Jackson, presidential action is most likely to be constitutional when there is at least some implicit congressional support.

Executive orders and other unilateral presidential actions can address a wide range of topics, both foreign and domestic. However, there is a distinctive tool—executive agreements—that presidents use to enter into international agreements without going through the treaty approval process described by the Constitution. The Supreme Court has given executive agreements the same legal standing as treaties, meaning that presidents can unilaterally enter into a binding executive agreement with another country without gaining the two-thirds approval by the Senate required for treaties. Presidents since the mid-twentieth century have used executive agreements to conclude nearly all international agreements. Critics claim that this simply allows presidents to bypass the constitutional process for treaty approval. Some scholars, however, conclude that the use of executive agreements does not go so far—after all, presidents still submit some proposed international agreements to the Senate for approval, and Congress has constitutional tools to rein in a president who abuses the executive agreement mechanism.

Executive orders, executive agreements, and other unilateral actions are not a magic wand that presidents can wave to accomplish whatever they like. Under the Constitution, limits apply and can be set by the courts, Congress, or voters. However, these checks are not automatic: whether presidential power is used effectively, in a balanced and limited way, depends on whether others in a position to set limits take effective action.

About the author

Chris Edelson is an assistant professor of government at American University. His research focuses on U.S. presidential power.

Suggestions for further reading

In this book

See essays 14 (The President as Chief Executive), 15 (The Crucial Power to Appoint and Remove Officials), 16 (Who Really Makes the Laws?), and 29 (Is the Administrative State Unconstitutional?).

Elsewhere

Cooper, Philip J. 2014. *By Order of the President: The Use and Abuse of Executive Direct Action*. Lawrence: University Press of Kansas.

Krutz, Glen S., and Jeffrey S. Peake. 2009. *Treaty Politics and the Rise of Executive Agreements: International Commitments in a System of Shared Powers*. Ann Arbor: University of Michigan Press.

Mayer, Kenneth R. 2001. *With the Stroke of a Pen: Executive Orders and Presidential Power*. Princeton, NJ: Princeton University Press.

18
Can the President Start a War?

Rebecca U. Thorpe

In February 2021, President Joe Biden ordered air strikes against Iran-backed militias in Syria without conferring with Congress. Biden's military action drew criticism from Republicans and some Democrats in Congress, who said that they were not adequately consulted on the strikes and questioned Biden's legal authority. While these critics argued that the president requires explicit authorization from Congress in order to exercise military force, the White House claimed that the president's authority falls under his powers as "commander in chief."

Biden launched the air strikes despite this vocal opposition. Yet some of the president's other priorities—like improving the nation's infrastructure and protecting voting rights—have stalled because Congress would not approve the measures.

To readers familiar with presidential war powers, this outcome may not be surprising. But it should be. Biden's actions in Syria not only endangered civilian lives but also risked escalating the conflict and destabilizing the region. Why is it that presidents can take actions as consequential as launching air strikes overseas without congressional notification, deliberation, or approval but cannot advance core components of their domestic agenda without congressional cooperation?

In approaching this question, we need to recognize that the Constitution grants specific war powers to both Congress and the president. Article II designates the president "commander in chief" of the armed forces, while Article I vests Congress with the power "to declare war," "raise and support armies," and "provide and maintain a navy." The greater specificity in Article I could be read to suggest that Congress has an essential role in deciding whether to go to war, and some early practice and court decisions were consistent with that reading. But the historical trend has been toward presidential dominance, and this trend has been driven by congressional and presidential practice, not by court decisions.

From the beginning, U.S. presidents have sought to steer the course of the nation's foreign and military policy. However, earlier presidents faced significant resource constraints. For most of the nation's history, Congress increased military spending only in preparation for specific wars and dismantled the military immediately after the conflict. Consequently, presidents relied on Congress to mobilize armies and finance their military ventures.

This all changed during and after World War II. The United States emerged from the war as an economic and military superpower. As the nation confronted new national security prerogatives, Congress maintained large armies and prioritized continued investments in military technology. Hundreds of defense industries that were created for wartime mobilization became a permanent fixture of the nation's industrial and technological base.

In this new context, the U.S. military is not only the most powerful in history but also incomparably the most expensive—and members of Congress work aggressively to maintain it. Republican- and Democratic-controlled Congresses and administrations since World War II have routinely spent more on the military than on every other item in the discretionary budget added together. Today the United States spends nearly as much on the military as the rest of the world combined.

President Truman was the first to take advantage of this new reality. Referring to the Korean War as a "police action" (using a semantic sleight of hand to explain the absence of a congressional declaration of war), he unilaterally committed the United States to a military conflict that would take four years to conclude. Since then, Congresses have furnished presidents with the armies, weapons systems, and funding to wage war at a moment's notice.

Of course, presidents are still responsive to voters, and public opinion constrains how they exercise military force overseas. However, just as Congress has invested in large supplies of arms and armies, a diminishing percentage of Americans are actually involved with the military.

Historically, most American citizens experienced the burdens and hardship of war by enlisting in the armed forces, fighting and dying in military conflicts, paying higher taxes in wartime, and incurring disruptions to peacetime life. However, the elimination of the military draft in 1973 transformed military service from a widely shared civic duty to a voluntary option. Since then, the burden of serving multiple overseas deployments has fallen disproportionately on the poor, less educated, and communities of color. At the same time, increasing reliance on private military and security contractors in U.S. war zones decreases the number of volunteers needed to fight wars overseas. Greater use of unmanned technologies, or drones, makes it possible to engage in overseas conflicts without even placing American lives at risk. Finally, as budgets increasingly roll into deficit spending, policymakers can support large defense budgets and wage war without raising taxes or demanding financial sacrifices from American citizens. This process of outsourcing military functions makes the country more willing to exercise military force overseas and more disengaged from debates over American foreign policy.

Legal scholars still disagree about the proper scope of the president's constitutional authority to wage war. However, presidents can effectively launch military actions without congressional authorization or democratic deliberation as long as Congress provides an uninterrupted source of funding. Presidents can also anticipate public support for (or tolerance of) their actions as long as most Americans are not directly affected. As actions from Truman's undeclared war in Korea to Biden's air strikes in Syria show, this new context frees presidents to formulate and carry out their military agendas independently.

About the author

Rebecca U. Thorpe is an associate professor of political science at the University of Washington, Seattle. Her research focuses on institutional development and state violence.

Suggestions for further reading

In this book
See essay 57 (Does the Constitution Work in a Crisis?).

Elsewhere
Youngstown Sheet & Tube Co. v. Sawyer, 343 U.S. 579 (1952).

Howell, Will. 2013. *Thinking about the Presidency: The Primacy of Power.* Princeton, NJ: Princeton University Press.

19

How Can We Get Rid of a Bad President?

Donald A. Zinman

Removing an ineffective, unfit, or lawless president by way of an election is difficult enough. There is a default tendency to give the current president the benefit of the doubt and reelect him. In addition, the political and institutional advantages of incumbency create a significant hurdle for any challenger in an election.

To constitutionally remove an ineffective, unfit, or lawless president before the next election is even more arduous. Impeachment and the Twenty-Fifth Amendment both provide pathways for doing so, but each approach comes with barriers that make these unrealistic methods for getting rid of a defective chief executive, except under the most extraordinary circumstances.

Impeachment of a president is authorized in Article II under the standards of "Treason, Bribery, or Other High Crimes and Misdemeanors." The process must begin in the House of Representatives, where the vote of a simple majority of members who are present is required for the passage of an article of impeachment. While it is plausible that a partisan majority in the House could impeach a president of the opposition party upon blatantly political grounds, in reality, this would be an unlikely scenario unless relations between the White House and the legislative branch were to become especially toxic. On the other hand, as the constitutional standards for impeachment are vague and subject to flexible interpretation by elected members of Congress, the possibility exists that a controversial or unpopular president could at least be impeached by the House.

Impeachment, however, does not remove a president from office. The Constitution requires a Senate trial, where evidence against the accused is heard, arguments are made, and witnesses may testify. Senators sit as jurors and even have to take a separate oath before the trial begins. An affirmative vote of two-thirds is required to convict and remove the president from office. If the accused is convicted, the Senate, by a simple majority vote, then has the option to disqualify that person from ever holding federal office. This is an important guardrail to prevent a dangerous politician, who nonetheless may still enjoy some degree of popular support, from once again infiltrating the United States government.

While the Constitution calls this procedure a trial, that is a bit of a misnomer, given that nobody is being tried for a crime. Nor does an impeachment proceeding require the same rules of procedure and evidentiary standards as a criminal trial. Indeed, the Constitution specifies that the impeached officeholder is still subject to possible criminal indictment in the future. No president in American history has ever been removed from office by way of a Senate impeachment trial. A two-thirds vote requirement for conviction requires a bipartisan buy-in, which will be very difficult to achieve unless there is significant popular support in the nation. Those conditions likely existed during the latter months of the Watergate scandal of President Richard Nixon, but he resigned in August 1974, thereby ending the impeachment process.

The Twenty-Fifth Amendment explicates the process for removing—if maybe only temporarily—a president who is unfit to perform their constitutional duties. The intent of this amendment was to provide a mechanism for filling vacancies in the vice presidency and to ensure continuity of government if the president were to become incapacitated (most likely due to a health emergency). While the text of the amendment is lengthy and detailed, many hypothetical questions remain if this provision were to ever be used to remove a president from office involuntarily.

The Twenty-Fifth Amendment can be utilized if a president is deemed "unable to discharge the powers and duties of his office." This will not be controversial or difficult if a president personally certifies to these facts. President Ronald Reagan, for example, invoked the Twenty-Fifth Amendment for a few hours on July 13, 1985, because he was undergoing colon cancer surgery. Vice President George H. W. Bush assumed the full powers of the presidency during that time, and Reagan then signed a letter stating that he was ready to perform his duties once again.

But what if a president is unfit to do the job and resists demands that he or she step aside? The text spells out the procedures for an involuntary invocation of the Twenty-Fifth Amendment. At that point, the vice president and a majority in the cabinet must vote to deem the president unfit. The president, however, can challenge that conclusion, which would leave the controversy for Congress to resolve. A two-thirds majority would have to certify the president as unfit to do the job, which would require some level of bipartisan agreement, revealing that this outcome is at least as daunting as removal by impeachment.

There has never been an involuntary invocation of the Twenty-Fifth Amendment to remove a president, which raises questions about the circumstances for using these provisions. Many dark scenarios are possible. What if a dangerously mentally ill president began to make arbitrary threats to launch nuclear weapons? Before the removal process could be completed, the missiles may have already been deployed. What if the cabinet began the process to invoke the Twenty-Fifth Amendment, but upon hearing this, the president immediately fired all the cabinet secretaries before they could do their work? What if the votes to remove the president are not to be found in the cabinet? Most of these men and women are quite loyal to their boss and would be loath to cross the president publicly.

Finally, what constitutes a president who is unfit to serve? Why not use the impeachment process or wait for the next election? A national debate to consider possible revisions and the proper use of the Twenty-Fifth Amendment is badly needed.

About the author

Donald A. Zinman is a professor of political science at Grand Valley State University in Allendale, Michigan. His research interests include the presidency and American political development.

Suggestions for further reading

In this book
See essays 14 (The President as Chief Executive), 15 (The Crucial Power to Appoint and Remove Officials), and 20 (Judicial Review).

Elsewhere
Brettschneider, Corey. 2018. *The Oath and the Office: A Guide to the Constitution for Future Presidents*. New York: W. W. Norton.

Tribe, Laurence, and Joshua Matz. 2018. *To End a Presidency: The Power of Impeachment*. New York: Basic Books.

Wineapple, Brenda. 2019. *The Impeachers: The Trial of Andrew Johnson and the Dream of a Just Nation*. New York: Random House.

20
Judicial Review

Allyson Yankle

After suffering massive electoral losses, the majority party in government acts quickly to tighten its hold on the judiciary before leaving office. Acts are signed, and new judgeships are created. But the majority party gets sloppy and fails to make sure the new judges are seated before the new administration takes office. One of the newly appointed judges who doesn't get his seat, William Marbury, takes advantage of an earlier law. This law allows cases like Marbury's to bypass lower courts and go directly to the U.S. Supreme Court but appears to be contradicted by the Constitution. Can the Supreme Court hear Marbury's case even if the law he is using to pursue the case seems to go against the Constitution? And more importantly, who gets to decide what the Constitution allows and doesn't allow?

The Constitution itself provides no answers to these questions. Article III, which discusses the federal judiciary, is a paltry 377 words with seemingly important details missing. One such missing detail is which branch gets to decide what the Constitution means. In *Marbury v. Madison* (1803), the Supreme Court answered this question. Claiming the power of judicial review, the Supreme Court established that it has the power to decide whether a state or federal law is constitutional or not.

Over time, the Court has reinforced its supremacy as interpreter of the Constitution. Consider the case of *Cooper v. Aaron* (1958), where state officials in Arkansas argued they did not have to obey federal court orders requiring desegregation after *Brown v. Board of Education* (1954). In response, the Supreme Court reasserted that its interpretations of the Constitution are "the supreme Law of the Land." Other government officials, whether local, state, or federal, are bound to respect the Court's interpretations of the Constitution unless the Court changes its mind or the Constitution is amended.

This assertion and exercise of power are not without critics. For some, the issue is straightforward. Because judicial review is not mentioned in the Constitution, it is not a legitimate form of judicial power. Others wrestle with the potential consequences of judicial review as a power within a constitutional democracy. Article III allows federal judges to stay on the bench as long as they want, unless they are impeached. This relieves the federal judiciary of pressure from other officials and the whims of the electorate. But this means that the judiciary's checks on the other two branches of government come with limited input from the democratic process (save for the nomination and confirmation process).

Judicial review also allows the Supreme Court to insert itself into hotly contested debates on national issues. Should the federal government be allowed to tax individual income? Who counts as an American citizen? Can states ban abortion? Can someone be prosecuted for burning the American flag in protest? All of these questions have been answered by the Supreme Court and have caused political ripples across the country. After the Court has decided these cases, it takes either a reversal in precedent or an amendment to the Constitution—not an easy feat—to overturn the decision.

On the other hand, many view judicial review as a necessary check on the other two branches of government, which would be too powerful if they also had the power to decide the Constitution's meaning. Others note that the power to interpret the Constitution is best left to the judiciary, as judges have often spent their lives learning about the law and interpreting legal principles. Judicial review is merely an extension of this specialized training. Finally, the Supreme Court does not have the ability to execute its own decisions, which represents a tremendous limitation to its power.

The power of judicial review and the Supreme Court's role as an authoritative interpreter of the Constitution are generally accepted by the American public. Historically, surveys have shown that Americans are trusting and supportive of the Court even following controversial decisions where judicial review was used. While public support for the Court has been declining, it is generally more supported and trusted than the other two branches of the federal government. This suggests that even with the concerns about the Supreme Court's power and use of judicial review, judicial review continues to be seen as a legitimate power.

Beginning in *Marbury v. Madison* (1803), the Supreme Court has claimed the power to decide what the Constitution means and to nullify laws that are inconsistent with its interpretation of the Constitution. There is some debate around the appropriateness and scope of the Court's authority, but the power is rarely challenged. Overall, both American society and the government have signaled their acceptance that, yes, the

Supreme Court has the power of judicial review, and yes, it is the final interpreter of the U.S. Constitution.

About the author

Allyson Yankle is an assistant professor of political science at Radford University. She works primarily on judicial ethics violations and judicial motivations.

Suggestions for further reading

In this book
See essays 6 (How Can We Tell What the Constitution Means?), 7 (Is the Constitution What the Justices Say It Is?), and 21 (The Challenge of Judicial Independence).

Elsewhere
The Federalist Papers nos. 78 and 80.

Bickel, Alexander M. 1986. *The Least Dangerous Branch: The Supreme Court at the Bar of American Politics*, 2nd ed. New Haven, CT: Yale University Press.

Waldron, Jeremy. 1999. "Banking Constitutional Rights: Who Controls Withdrawals?" *Arkansas Law Review* 52 (3): 533–62.

21
The Challenge of Judicial Independence

Charles Gardner Geyh

Imagine that you are part of a desert island community that has decided it needs a way to govern itself. And suppose that the group has decided to be governed by a system of laws made by the people themselves, because turning control of the island over to a single person would get dicey if that person became dictatorial. When disagreements arose over whether somebody had violated a given law, you would need people—judges—to apply the law and resolve those disagreements on a case-by-case basis. If you are serious about making sure that your judges resolve disputes on the basis of applicable facts and law, you will want to shield the judge from the control of those with an interest in the case, who could otherwise pressure the judge to contort the facts or law in their favor. At the same time, you don't want to insulate judges from external controls so completely that they are liberated to disregard the law and decide cases on the basis of their own ideological or other idiosyncratic predilections.

How to make judges independent of and yet accountable to the people they serve was a conundrum faced by those who drafted the U.S. Constitution. Judges in the American colonies had been rendered dependent on King George III, who controlled their tenure and salaries—a concern serious enough to be included among the grievances listed in the Declaration of Independence. To promote judicial independence, delegates to the Constitutional Convention were united in the view that judges should enjoy tenure during good behavior and a salary that could not be diminished and so stated in Article III, Section 1. At the same time, tenure during "good" behavior implied a corresponding need to hold judges accountable for bad behavior. The framers therefore established a process whereby judges could be impeached upon a majority vote in the House of Representatives and removed with a two-thirds majority vote in the Senate for "treason, bribery, or other high crimes and misdemeanors." Impeachment, Alexander

Hamilton declared in *The Federalist Papers*, was the "only" means the Constitution provided to ensure the "responsibility" of judges because it was the only means compatible with judicial independence.

But the drafters of the Constitution were focused on concerns related to the legislative and executive branches of the new government and gave the judiciary less time and attention. As a consequence, they largely overlooked other ways in which the Constitution effectively authorized Congress to call judges to task for their conduct at the expense of judicial independence. For example, Congress might exploit its power to establish lower courts by disestablishing courts whose decisions or judges it disfavored. It could wield its powers to tax and spend to slash the budgets of unpopular courts or hinge judicial salary increases on case outcomes. Congress could punish the Supreme Court for unwelcome rulings by stripping the Court's authority to hear cases on controversial subjects pursuant to its power to make exceptions to the Supreme Court's appellate jurisdiction. Or Congress could define impeachable crimes to include rulings it deemed high-handed and remove judges indiscriminately.

Although Congress has exploited some of these devices to curb the courts, particularly in the early years of the nation's history, it has for the most part stayed its hand. These encroachments have come to be regarded as antithetical to the independent judiciary that the framers sought to create, and over time, Congress has internalized informal conventions against taking such measures. The net effect is that the federal judiciary's independence has been more muscular in practice than the text of the Constitution requires.

Because the cumbersome impeachment process has succeeded in removing only eight federal judges in over 230 years and because Congress has been loath to control judicial decision-making by other means seemingly at its disposal, some argue that the federal judiciary is too independent and too unaccountable. Judicial accountability, however, is promoted in additional ways. Congress exercises general oversight of court budgets and operations. It has established a court structure that subjects judicial decisions to appeal and reversal, it has provided for the disqualification of judges whose impartiality is in doubt, and it has created a system of judicial discipline for the lower courts. Congress can pass laws overriding court interpretations of statutes, and it can introduce constitutional amendments to overturn court interpretations of the Constitution. The judiciary's governing body, the Judicial Conference of the United States, subjects lower court judges to a code of ethical conduct. And the courts themselves are mindful of the powers that Congress holds in reserve and avoid unnecessary confrontations.

Those concerned that the federal judiciary is insufficiently accountable have a stronger argument when it comes to the Supreme Court.

No Supreme Court justice has ever been removed by impeachment, the justices are not subject to a code of conduct or a disciplinary process, each justice has the final say over her or his own disqualification, the Supreme Court's decisions are not subject to appellate review, and amending the Constitution is so difficult that only four Supreme Court decisions have been directly overturned by constitutional amendment in the nation's history. Perhaps in part because the Supreme Court is more independent and less accountable for its conduct, social scientists have documented a more robust correlation between the votes that Supreme Court justices cast and their ideological preferences, relative to circuit and district judges.

The future of the federal judiciary's independence is rendered precarious by the polarized age in which we live, where public confidence in the federal government is low, distrust of judges appointed by presidents of the disfavored political party is high, and the impulse to control the ideological orientation of the federal courts is considerable. In the near term, at least, one can anticipate the possibility that long-standing conventions against congressional encroachment on the judiciary's autonomy are likely to be challenged with greater intensity than in generations past.

About the author

Charles Gardner Geyh is Indiana University Distinguished Professor and John F. Kimberling Professor of Law at the Indiana University Maurer School of Law. His research focuses on judicial ethics, administration, independence, and selection.

Suggestions for further reading

In this book
See essays 6 (How Can We Tell What the Constitution Means?), 7 (Is the Constitution What the Justices Say It Is?), and 20 (Judicial Review).

Elsewhere
Gerber, Scott Douglas. 2011. *A Distinct Judicial Power: The Origins of an Independent Judiciary, 1606–1787*. New York: Oxford University Press.

Geyh, Charles Gardner. 2006. *When Courts and Congress Collide: The Struggle for Control of America's Judicial System*. Ann Arbor: University of Michigan Press.

Peabody, Bruce, ed. 2011. *The Politics of Judicial Independence: Courts, Politics, and the Public*. Baltimore, MD: Hopkins University Press.

Representative Democracy

22
Who Can Vote?

Greg W. Vonnahme

What does the Constitution say about who can vote? Not much. The Constitution is an exceptionally short document: 4,543 words long. The original, unamended text of the Constitution says that there will be elections but says very little about how those elections are to function. The Constitution left most of those decisions to state legislatures:

- The right to vote in House elections is determined by state legislatures.
- The time, place, and manner of federal elections were left to the states, although the Constitution reserves power for congressional regulation.
- State legislatures determine the manner of choosing presidential electors.

When the system of constitutional government began in 1789, that was the constitutional landscape concerning the right to vote. The deference to state legislatures is unsurprising given the unique institutional context of the Constitution. States preceded the federal government, and most of the framers had political experience in state legislatures. Early American elections had numerous voting exclusions, including racial/ethnic groups, sex, religious qualifications, and wealth/property requirements, among others.

The right to vote has expanded gradually and greatly since that time. While the Constitution has only been amended seventeen times since 1791, six of those amendments directly apply to the right to vote more than any other single topic. These amendments come in the form of proscriptions that constrain state legislatures and expand the right to vote. They extend voting rights to more people and expand the number of elected offices. These amendments are the following:

- prohibition on racial exclusions (Fifteenth Amendment, 1870)
- direct election of senators (Seventeenth Amendment, 1913)
- women's suffrage (Nineteenth Amendment, 1920)
- Electoral College representation for Washington, DC (Twenty-Third Amendment, 1961)
- Allowing residents of Washington, DC, to vote in presidential elections (Twenty-Third Amendment, 1961)
- prohibition on poll taxes (Twenty-Fourth Amendment, 1964)
- allowing eighteen-year-olds to vote (Twenty-Sixth Amendment, 1971)

The political implications of these amendments are enormous. They expanded the American electorate from a small proportion of the population to a system of elections in which almost every adult citizen had a constitutionally guaranteed right to vote. States have recently revisited the issue of felon disenfranchisement. Felons often lose their voting rights while incarcerated. Whether and how those rights are restored upon release varies from state to state. Different states have different rules covering whether restoration is possible and, if so, whether it is automatic or requires an additional application process and if restoration is allowed immediately upon release or is subject to other conditions, such as parole or paying any remaining fines or fees.

The history of the American franchise has a complex and uneven trajectory. The Constitution has had broader implications than just the direct proscriptions on discriminatory practices. In 1944, the U.S. Supreme Court decided the case *Smith v. Allwright*. The issue in this case was the validity of "white primaries." Southern states at that time were one-party dominant states, where there was no competitive Republican Party, and so the only meaningful electoral competition was in the Democratic primaries. State Democratic parties in the South adopted racially exclusive primary elections, arguing that primary elections were simply party functions. They were activities of "private clubs" that were not bound by the same constitutional strictures as general elections. The effect of these practices was to deny Black voters meaningful access to the polls. In 1944, the Supreme Court ruled that these practices were violations of the Fourteenth Amendment's equal protection clause and the Fifteenth Amendment.

The right to vote involves issues of not only vote *denial* but also vote *dilution*. Vote dilution is a more insidious problem because it involves the manner in which votes are aggregated, not explicit limits on who can vote. Dilution strategies allowed voters to participate but engineered electoral rules to limit how those votes translated into representation. Vote dilution has taken many forms, but the Supreme Court has ruled that the Constitution prohibits malapportionment, which is one significant method of vote dilution. In a series of cases in the early 1960s (*Baker v. Carr*, 1962; *Wesberry v. Sanders*, 1964; and *Reynolds v. Sims*, 1964), the Supreme Court ruled that the Fourteenth Amendment's equal protection clause prohibits unequally sized legislative districts. These rulings applied to U.S. House and state legislative districts. These decisions established a constitutional protection from certain vote dilution strategies that had created disparities in voting.

The Constitution also allows Congress to regulate the conduct of elections. One of the most important pieces of federal legislation is the Voting Rights Act of 1965, which created a system of standards and practices to prevent racial/ethnic minority vote dilution. In 2013, the Supreme Court invalidated part of the Voting Rights Act in its *Shelby County v. Holder* decision. Congress has regulated elections on numerous other occasions, including the following:

- establishing the first Tuesday after the first Monday in November as Election Day
- requiring the use of single-member districts for House seats
- enacting the *Uniformed and Overseas Citizens Absentee Voting Act* and the *Military and Overseas Voter Empowerment Act*, which regulate elections for civilians and members of the military that are overseas
- Passing the *National Voter Registration Act*, which is aimed at expanding voter registration
- Implementing the *Help America Vote Act*, which requires that states modernize voting equipment and set accessibility standards for disabled voters

While constitutional amendments and federal legislation have significantly expanded the right to vote, state legislatures retain significant discretion over the administration of elections. Most of the "times, places, and manners" decisions about elections are still made by state legislatures. Often, state legislatures delegate those decisions to local authorities. Most of those are county officials, which has created a patchwork of voting practices regarding where, when, and how people vote. There are over seven thousand local election jurisdictions in the United States, each with its own practices. While almost all adult Americans have a constitutionally protected right to vote, how that actually operates in terms of in-person early voting, vote by mail, ID requirements, signature requirements, provisional balloting standards, registration and residency deadlines, automatic registration, electronic voting, types of voting equipment, polling places, and availability of poll workers varies significantly.

About the author

Greg W. Vonnahme is the department chair and associate professor of political science at the University of Missouri-Kansas City. His research focuses on election administration and state politics and policy.

Suggestions for further reading

In this book
See essays 40 (How Did the Civil War Amendments Change the Constitution?), 41 (Who Is a Citizen?), and 43 (Does the Equal Protection Clause Cover Gender?).

Elsewhere
Keyssar, Alexander. 2009. *The Right to Vote: The Contested History of Democracy in the United States*. New York: Basic Books.

Election Law Blog. http://electionlawblog.org/—*Election Law Blog: The Law of Politics and the Politics of Law*.

Caltech / MIT Voting Technology Project. http://www.vote.caltech.edu.

23
Why Is My Congressional District Such a Weird Shape?

Jeffrey L. Bernstein

> Representatives and direct Taxes shall be apportioned among the several States which may be included within this Union, according to their respective Numbers. The actual Enumeration shall be made within three Years after the first Meeting of the Congress of the United States, and within every subsequent Term of ten Years.
>
> —U.S. Constitution, Article I, Section 2, Clause 3

> The Times, Places and Manner of holding Elections for Senators and Representatives, shall be prescribed in each State by the Legislature thereof; but the Congress may at any time by Law make or alter such Regulations, except as to the Places of chusing Senators.
>
> —U.S. Constitution, Article I, Section 4

Before you read this essay, Google "Goofy Kicking Donald Duck." You will see a map of what used to be the Seventh Congressional District of Pennsylvania, which looks like, well, Goofy kicking Donald Duck. This is just one example among many ridiculously shaped congressional districts. How did we end up with such districts? And to what effect?

The Constitution requires that congressional representation be apportioned according to the numbers within each state every ten years. Easy enough. It proceeds to give Congress and the states the ability to determine how representatives should be chosen. States have traditionally chosen to elect representatives in single-member districts; these single-member districts have been required by federal law since the 1967 passage of Public

Law 90–196, which required no more than one representative to be elected from each congressional district. By requiring states to create and recreate districts to ensure that the state has one separate district for each representative it is apportioned, this choice opened up a Pandora's box.

The courts have offered some guidance over the years. Early court decisions, such as *Wesberry v. Sanders* (1964) and *Karcher v. Daggett* (1983), ordered that these districts be of equal population "as nearly as is practicable." In *Shaw v. Reno* (1993) and *Miller v. Johnson* (1995), the Supreme Court ruled that race could not be the principal factor in how districts were drawn. While the courts have struck down districts that focused on race in drawing boundaries, they have not chosen to do that in cases of extreme partisan gerrymandering, ruling in *Rucho v. Common Cause* (2019) that these were political questions best left to legislatures to decide.

What does this mean in a practical sense? Imagine two states. In the first, the parties have divided control of the state government—perhaps one party holds the state legislature, while the other controls the governorship. In a traditional arrangement, where district lines are proposed by the legislature and approved by the governor, neither party can press an advantage. When this is the case, we might see a map that protects incumbent officeholders of each party. Perhaps a Democratic representative might "give" Republican territory in their district to a neighboring Republican, who might in turn "trade back" Democratic areas in their district to the Democrat. Incumbents benefit; the only losers here are the voters, who are likely to see fewer and fewer competitive House districts remaining.

Now imagine a second state, in which one party controls both the governorship and the state legislature. Here, the dominant party may engage in a partisan process, in which they attempt to pack as many of the opposing party's likely voters into a few districts and distribute the remainder in order to give themselves a majority in as many districts as possible. This type of line drawing also reduces the number of competitive districts but this time in a partisan manner, favoring one party over the other.

This process of drawing district lines to promote certain electoral outcomes is known as gerrymandering. (The name comes from a district in Massachusetts, which was drawn for political purposes by Elbridge *Gerry* and happened to look like a *salamander*. Hence gerrymandering.) Gerrymandering can lead to weirdly shaped districts, like Goofy Kicking Donald Duck.

In addition to making congressional elections less competitive in most districts, gerrymandering also changes the incentives of members of Congress. In a district with a roughly equal number of Democrats and

Republicans, members of Congress are likely to fear a general election defeat. This may lead them to reach out to a broad range of their constituents in order to minimize strong challenges from the other party. As districts become less competitive, members no longer fear general election defeat as much as they fear losing in a primary. Since the voters who vote in primaries tend to be on the ideological extremes of each party, one result of heavily gerrymandered districts is candidates who are pulled to the ideological poles of their party and hence fear compromise with the opposite party. This is an important explanation for increased partisan polarization in Congress.

The existence of gerrymandering should not be a surprise—political parties are self-interested actors and are likely to pursue a partisan advantage whenever they can. One way to prevent gerrymandering is to limit the parties' ability to participate in redistricting. The state of Arizona has created an Independent Redistricting Commission, with an aim to take the parties out of the process of drawing district lines and restore more fairness to the process. This practice was sanctioned by the Supreme Court in *Arizona State Legislature v. Arizona Independent Redistricting Commission* (2015), in which the Court ruled that state legislatures may delegate the task of drawing lines to these independent commissions. Other states have followed Arizona and created similar commissions. Their supporters hope these commissions will restore competition to congressional elections and help erase some of the partisan polarization that exists in Washington.

Independent commissions may well create districts that better reflect the population of the state and may take the political gamesmanship out of the process. They are unlikely, however, to produce districts as visually interesting as the ones produced by our political parties!

About the author

Jeffrey L. Bernstein is a professor of political science and director of the Bruce K. Nelson Faculty Development Center at Eastern Michigan University. His work focuses primarily on civic education and the scholarship of teaching and learning.

Suggestions for further reading

In this book
See essays 25 (Why Do Wyoming and California Have the Same Number of Senators?) and 27 (Can the Constitution Handle Political Parties?).

Elsewhere

Allen, Brooke Thomas. 2020. "Gerrymandering as Art: A New Method for Teaching Redistricting." *Journal of Political Science Education* 17 (1): 1–11. https://doi.org/10.1080/15512169.2020.1854773.

Bullock, Charles S., III. 2021. *Redistricting: The Most Political Activity in America*, 2nd ed. Lanham, MD: Rowman and Littlefield.

Engstrom, Richard L. 2020. "Partisan Gerrymandering: Weeds in the Political Thicket." *Social Science Quarterly* 101 (1): 23–36. https://online library.wiley.com/doi/10.1111/ssqu.12743.

Kury, Franklin L. 2018. *Gerrymandering: A Guide to Congressional Redistricting, Dark Money, and the U.S. Supreme Court*. Lanham, MD: Rowman and Littlefield.

24
Is the Electoral College Undemocratic?

Sheahan Virgin

Hours into election night 2016, Donald Trump faced a sobering reality: he would win a majority in the Electoral College—and thus the presidency—despite having received fewer popular votes than his rival, Hillary Rodham Clinton. Trump's opponents pounced, portraying his election as illegitimate, the result of a malfunctioning electoral system that had subverted democracy. "If we really subscribe to the notion that [the] 'majority rules,'" opined Jennifer Granholm, the former governor of Michigan, "then why do we deny the majority their [*sic*] chosen candidate?"

Critics of the Electoral College harbor many grievances against the institution, but they reserve singular condemnation for the occurrence of a "wrong-winner president" (or "inverted election"), defined as a split between the decisions rendered by the aggregate popular vote and the Electoral College. How, they ask, can a country that fashions itself as the world's premiere democracy accept the most undemocratic of outcomes: the ascension to office of an individual whom most voters did not support?

In modern times, we equate democracy with "the people rule." Sure, they let politicians do the policy-making, but importantly, this authority belongs to the mass public, not elites: the former temporarily leases its power to govern to the latter. This framework, call it the "democratic bargain," positions the people as principals who select agents via elections. Once in office, an agent should pursue the interests of the principals that put her there; if she misbehaves (pursues her own goals, pursues the people's goals but ineffectively), she may get the boot at the next election.

With an inverted election, there is the unseemly appearance of the democratic bargain upended; after all, the agent-elect is an individual whom the principals, in the aggregate, had not intended to authorize.

Many Americans do not understand how, mechanically, the Electoral College produces a "wrong winner," a lack of knowledge that degrades the national discourse over the desirability of retaining the Electoral College. The answer is that an inverted election is a function of two seemingly benign characteristics of the electoral system: (1) the partitioning of the national electorate into fifty-one subnational jurisdictions (fifty states plus DC) and (2) the decision by forty-nine of those jurisdictions to allocate their electors as an indivisible, winner-takes-all bundle (unit rule)—thus, the candidate with the most votes in a state nabs all of its electors, no matter the margin.

As a teacher, I have found that students respond well to a fictitious example that, because it only uses four states, is more manageable, arithmetically. First, suppose the following:

- State a: 200 voters, 20 electors to the college
- State b: 150 voters, 15 electors
- State c: 100 voters, 10 electors
- State d: 100 voters, 10 electors

The college thus comprises 55 electors, a majority of which is 28; whichever candidate hits this threshold wins. Second, suppose each state uses unit rule. Finally, our candidates: old foes Thomas Jefferson and Alexander Hamilton, who loathe each other. All 550 voters cast their ballots, yielding the following:

- State a: 101 votes Jefferson (50.5%), 99 Hamilton (49.5%)
- State b: 50 votes Jefferson (33.3%), 100 Hamilton (66.7%)
- State c: 52 votes Jefferson (52.0%), 48 Hamilton (48.0%)
- State d: 20 votes Jefferson (20.0%), 80 Hamilton (80.0%)

The aggregate popular vote, then, is 223 Jefferson (40.5%) to 327 Hamilton (59.5%), a Hamilton landslide. Or is it?

Because the electoral system is the college, the calculations above are a beauty contest. Turning now to the count that matters:

- State a, 20 electors to Jefferson
- State b, 15 electors to Hamilton
- State c, 10 electors to Jefferson
- State d, 10 electors to Hamilton

The aggregate electoral vote, then, is 30 Jefferson (54.5%) to 25 Hamilton (45.5%), a Jefferson landslide.

Furious, Hamilton's supporters ask him, "What fate hath befallen thee?" The answer: his support was distributed inefficiently across the states. His massive margins in b and d "wasted" votes, because in each, he only needed to best Jefferson barely for unit rule to activate. Conversely, his losses in a and c were narrow, yet as the second-place candidate, unit rule deprived him. The rules forbid it, but shift just three Hamilton voters from b to a, and a goes for Hamilton—he wins the college 45 to 10.

The same happened to Clinton in 2016: she padded her aggregate popular vote margin with landslides in populous Democratic strongholds like California and New York but lost squeakers throughout the industrial Midwest. But the rules didn't allow Clinton to transfer 23,000 of her 4.27 million "surplus" California votes to Wisconsin (10 electors), 11,000 to Michigan (16), and 45,000 to Pennsylvania (20), and so the result was a "wrong-winner."

It is important to appreciate, however, that the contemporary, democratic view of the office—that the president must be an agent of the people—diverges considerably from the position the framers created in 1787. Their mission was to achieve balance between their twin fears of an executive accountable to no one and an executive accountable to everyone. The former risked tyranny; the latter demagoguery.

Their solution was to innovate. To avoid a would-be king, they required the executive to obtain office via periodic elections. But as we saw above, an election begs the question of who, exactly, will do the electing. Believing the masses to be impulsive and uninformed, the framers opted against vesting the power of selection in them, opting rather for the Electoral College. This institution was to be a body of "wise and learned elders" who, though attuned to the interests of the people, would scrutinize the candidates to weed out any would-be demagogue.

Today, even proponents of the Electoral College concede that, due to the democratizing waves of the nineteenth and twentieth centuries—which, by expanding the franchise, revolutionized democratic governance—a president intentionally isolated from the people, as the framers sought, is inappropriate. The question is, then, if we accept that the president should be popularly elected by the people, then why retain an institution that was forged 230 years ago for an entirely different purpose?

About the author

Sheahan Virgin is an assistant professor of political science at Grinnell College in Grinnell, Iowa. His research focuses on the extrapartisan reasons elites and members of the mass public may decide either to support or oppose electoral reforms.

Suggestions for further reading

In this book
See essays 19 (How Can We Get Rid of a Bad President?), 23 (Why Is My Congressional District Such a Weird Shape?), and 59 (Does the Amendment Process Need Amendment?).

Elsewhere
Dahl, Robert A. 1998. *On Democracy*. New Haven, CT: Yale University Press. See esp. chaps. 4–8.

Edwards, George C., III. 2019. *Why the Electoral College Is Bad for America*, 3rd ed. New Haven, CT: Yale University Press. See esp. chaps. 2, 3, and 5.

Virgin, Sheahan G. 2017. "Competing Loyalties in Electoral Reform: An Analysis of the U.S. Electoral College." *Electoral Studies* 49:38–48.

25
Why Do Wyoming and California Have the Same Number of Senators?

Benjamin Kassow

> The Senate of the United States shall be composed of two Senators from each State, chosen by the Legislature thereof, for six Years; and each Senator shall have one Vote.
> —U.S. Constitution, Article I, Section 3

The framers' decision to give each state the same number of senators was an integral part of the Connecticut Compromise proposed by Roger Sherman and Oliver Ellsworth. States' seats in the House of Representatives were to be allocated according to population, and the smaller states (like Connecticut) feared that they would be unable to protect their interests against the more populous ones. Providing each state with the same number of senators would give smaller states the ability to counteract the larger states' influence in the lower house.

It is hard to guess what the framers would think of their decision today. Equal representation in the Senate certainly has provided protection to less populous states. However, it seems unlikely that the framers could have anticipated the huge disparities in population that we see today. Consider that Wyoming, with a population of approximately 550,000, has the same say in the Senate as California, with 39,000,000 residents. The twenty-five smallest states by population—which, of course, have half of the votes in the U.S. Senate—represent only 16 percent of the U.S. population. Today, small states have an influence in the Senate far out of proportion to their populations.

This institutional design has important effects on both politics and policies. Equal representation forces the Senate to address the interests and preferences of the less populated, more rural states. And if one political party performs especially strongly in these states, that party, too, will have disproportionate power in Congress. The advantaged party changes over time, but in recent years, it is the Republican Party that has benefited.

The same advantages operate to a lesser degree in presidential elections. This advantage exists because the number of electors per state is its combined number of U.S. House of Representatives members and senators. (Washington, DC, was given three electors in the Twenty-Third Amendment to the U.S. Constitution.)

In the Senate itself, the influence of small states is magnified by the filibuster, a rule that allows a minority of the Senate to block it from taking action. Since 1975, the Senate's rules have required a vote of three-fifths of all senators to invoke cloture, ending a filibuster. (Prior to 1975, the cloture threshold was two-thirds of all senators present.) Importantly, the filibuster is *not* found in the Constitution itself but is simply an internal rule of the Senate that can be removed with the votes of fifty-one senators. (There is an open question as to whether the vice president's tie breaker vote applies to Senate rules, as the vice president is not a sitting senator.)

Yet another feature of the Senate that affects the distribution of influence is our election of senators at large rather than in districts. Because all of a state's voters get to choose *both* its senators, a small but cohesive majority can monopolize that state's representation in the Senate.

Combined, these features have powerful effects, both for good and bad. On the bad side, they doubtless contributed to the dilution of African American voters' influence in the post-Reconstruction South, acted as a barrier against African American representation, and held back progress toward equal rights for many years. Congress was unable to take serious effective action on civil rights until the Civil Rights Act of 1964 and the Voting Rights Act of 1965.

On the good side, the Senate's unique structure can provide laudable protection for minority views and interests that might otherwise get overwhelmed by national majorities. It promotes a balance of power between more urban and less urban states and larger and smaller states and can induce states and interest groups to work toward consensus. Whether in the end you applaud the equal representation of states in the Senate or think it unfair, there is no denying that it deeply influences our politics.

About the author

Benjamin Kassow is an associate professor of political science at the University of North Dakota. His research examines how judges write opinions, as well as how judges use court precedents, broadly defined.

Suggestions for further reading

In this book
See essays 2 (Who Wrote the Constitution?), 24 (Is the Electoral College Undemocratic?), and 58 (Does the Constitution Cause Gridlock?).

Elsewhere
HR 1. 2021. "The For the People Act: How Can It Pass the Senate?" Vox. Last modified May 12, 2021. https://www.vox.com/2021/5/12/22430970/hr1 -for-the-people-act-senate-manchin.

Katzenbach v. Morgan, 384 U.S. 641 (1966).

The Federalist Papers no. 62.

26

Term Lengths, Stability, and Responsiveness

Beth Henschen

It seems obvious. When flaws in the Articles of Confederation appear too serious to fix, start fresh. Design a government that "works," but make sure to guard against a concentration of power. Create a system in which powers are separately shared across branches of government. Remember that you are writing the rules for a representative democracy, so those who govern will need to be responsive to the people.

The delegates who met in Philadelphia in 1787 faced a daunting task. Determining that it was necessary to establish a viable executive and a national court, both lacking under the Articles, was only the beginning. Disagreements over how to reimagine Congress threatened to halt the convention. Meetings held to discuss the selection of those who would serve in the new government were fraught with indecision. Nothing was obvious.

Starting with the legislative branch, the delegates readily decided on a bicameral structure to lessen the chance of abuses by congressional majorities. There were bitter disagreements, however, over who would choose the legislators and how long they would serve. Eventually, the Great Compromise resolved disputes that at their core were about the exercise of power. The people would elect representatives to the lower chamber for two-year terms, a middle ground between initial proposals of one and three. Frequent elections in the House helped rationalize longer terms in the Senate for those who were worried about popular passions driving policy-making. Senators would have six-year terms, but those terms would be staggered, with one-third of them chosen every two years. This would contribute to stability and continuity while guarding against the rise of an aristocracy.

Directly electing members of the most numerous chamber might strengthen the people's goodwill toward the central government. State legislatures, however, would elect senators, a nod to the importance of states in this new federal arrangement. State population would provide the basis for the apportionment of seats in the House, a decision that brought slavery into the discussion. The compromise that counted slaves for purposes of determining representation, by a three-fifths ratio, enhanced Southern power. The smaller states insisted on equal representation in the upper chamber. Each state would send two senators to Congress.

Meandering conversations considered numerous options for choosing the president, including congressional selection, popular election, and multiple chief executives chosen from different regions. Figuring out how to remove a president—impeachment—was easier than deciding how to choose one in the first place.

In the end, the selection process blended several elements to attract the widest support. Each state would have as many electors as it had representatives and senators in Congress, and they would choose the president. Each state legislature would decide how to select that state's electors. The delegates compromised on a presidential term of four years, with an opportunity for reelection. The vice presidency, created to succeed a president who could not finish a term, was also the product of compromise.

The relative ease with which the delegates reached an agreement that the members of the judiciary should "hold their offices during good behaviour" to protect judicial independence was remarkable. It was not entirely clear, however, what that independence would mean in practical terms. Nor did the framers establish formal requirements for membership on the Supreme Court, as they had done for representatives, senators, and the president. Although delegates floated other ideas, the final decision was that, subject to Senate approval, the president would appoint the justices, whose numbers were unspecified.

Concerns over regional power, sincere differences of opinion, a desire to compromise, and no small measure of frustration, impatience, and exhaustion resulted in selection processes, constituencies, and term lengths that differed across institutions. That doesn't mean the original design has been left unchanged. Revisions to executive offices in the Twelfth, Twentieth, and Twenty-Fifth Amendments were primarily procedural. Amendments fifteen, nineteen, twenty-three, twenty-four, and twenty-six each expanded the electorate in some way, altering campaign strategies and reshaping ideas about responsiveness to the people.

A statute fixing the number of representatives at 435 means that political power in the House and electoral votes are at stake when reapportionment takes place after a census. Supporters of the Seventeenth Amendment hoped to reduce the influence of state party machines and powerful interests by allowing senators to appeal directly to the voters. The direct election of senators, however, has brought little change to the kinds of people who run for office, the role of money in their selection, or their responsiveness to constituents.

Attempts to impose term limits on representatives, senators, and justices have been unsuccessful. The Twenty-Second Amendment limiting the president to two terms, however, is significant. It means that unlike their counterparts in Congress and the courts, presidents feel the pressure of time.

Decisions made at the convention continue to shape contemporary politics. Every two years, a new Congress convenes, forged by the electoral decisions of the people. Though the concept of "constituency" has become more complicated and difficult to define, representatives and senators are responsive to those who choose them, much as the framers intended. Political parties have dramatically altered presidential nomination and election processes, yet the Electoral College system remains. Independence has become a hallmark of the judiciary. A representative democracy, reflecting the principle of checks and balances, has lasted. The choices of 1787 seem obvious.

About the author

Beth Henschen is a faculty member in the political science department at Eastern Michigan University. Much of her research has focused on the interaction between the Supreme Court and Congress.

Suggestions for further reading

In this book
See essays 3 (Human Nature and the Constitution), 5 (Emulation and Innovation in the Constitutional System), and 13 (What Is the Purpose of the Separation of Powers?).

Elsewhere
Jones, Charles O. 2016. *The American Presidency: A Very Short Introduction*, 2nd ed. New York: Oxford University Press.

Stewart, David O. 2007. *The Summer of 1787*. New York: Simon & Schuster.

Van Doren, Carl. 1948. *The Great Rehearsal*. New York: Viking Penguin.

27
Can the Constitution Handle Political Parties?

Michael Catalano

Writing about the need to ratify the proposed U.S. Constitution in *Federalist* no. 10, James Madison warned of the dangers of factions—groups of people who put their own passions or interests above those of other citizens or of the community as a whole. To Madison and the other framers, political parties were a prime example of dangerous factions, and the Constitution includes no discussion of or provision for them.

Yet political parties quickly occupied a central place in American politics. Indeed, nearly eight decades ago, political scientist E. E. Schattschneider observed that democracy anywhere is "unthinkable" without the existence of political parties. A quick survey of contemporary democracies shows that political parties operate in every one. A tension, therefore, exists between the deep concern the framers had regarding political parties and the necessity of political parties for democracies to function.

Despite this tension, the U.S. Constitution has sustained itself for over 230 years. The emergence of political parties rendered some parts of the U.S. Constitution ineffective. And yet most parts of the Constitution maintain their ability to resolve issues for which they were created, as political parties add to the Constitution's robustness.

The unforeseen emergence of political parties reduced or eliminated the effectiveness of portions of the Constitution that assumed strong institutional loyalty, as institutional loyalty was supplanted by party loyalty. Two specific examples are the Electoral College and the impeachment process. Both have played considerable roles in current events, meaning this oversight by the framers has real and important influence on our lives today.

Since the ratification of the Constitution, the U.S. has selected its president through indirect election by the electors of the Electoral College. Instead of selecting the president based on political considerations, electors were to judge candidates based on the qualifications of the individual. The framers intended that electors be detached from political influence (see *Federalist* no. 68). For instance, electors cannot hold national office; the framers believed this would insulate electors from conflicts of interest, especially ones that might be posed by foreign actors.

Nevertheless, electors have never cast their vote for a president based on an objective or unbiased review of qualifications and characteristics. Rather, electors have voted according to the wishes of the political party that selected them to be electors. This makes it impossible for electors to remain detached from politics in their decision-making.

Regarding impeachment, the framers appeared aware that the process could be negatively conditioned by rival factions. They wrestled with how to ensure that political actors would use impeachment as a serious disciplinary action against the most egregious violations of public trust rather than a political device to weaken one's opponents. *Federalist* no. 65 argued that the "greatest danger" to the impeachment process would be instances where political actors decided on impeachment and guilt based on faction strength (i.e., political party preferences) rather than the merit of the accusations. In each of the country's impeachment and trial proceedings, party affiliation was a strong (though not perfect) predictor of a member of Congress's vote. This indicates that the framers were right to worry that parties might render impeachment a political partisan rather than principled disciplinary action.

Despite these shortcomings, the Constitution has proven resilient enough to coexist with political parties for over 230 years. It has even been strengthened in some ways by the very presence of parties. An important reason is the federal structure of the U.S. political system, which extends to the political party system. Like government itself, political parties operate at the local, state, and national levels.

While the federal Constitution does not directly regulate political parties, state constitutions do have rules that constrain parties. These state provisions dictate how parties gain ballot access for their candidates, define how political parties can support their candidates and officeholders, and ultimately structure in part the policy that can be pursued by policymakers at all levels of government. In these ways, state constitutions act as a safeguard to help keep political parties from overwhelming the U.S. Constitution.

Furthermore, the parties nominate candidates for offices in their geographic area and provide resources to aid those candidates. While each level of party organization may overlap in supporting candidates and elected policymakers, state parties can act as an important (but unintended) check on national parties and policy, providing a balance of powers among different levels of government as intended by the constitution.

States and state parties value the stability the U.S. Constitution brings to them. State parties often have an incentive to make sure that national policymakers adhere to the U.S. Constitution. Conversely, national policymakers check with state party leaders to gauge the impact of policy on their state. Those policymakers who threaten instability to the Constitution may risk losing their party's nomination and resources for future elections.

The framers of the Constitution did not welcome political parties or anticipate how important they would turn out to be. And parties have rendered parts of the Constitution less effective or even ineffective. Overall, however, the U.S. Constitution has shown itself equipped to endure, and even thrive, in the presence of political parties.

About the author

Michael Catalano is a PhD candidate in political science at SUNY Binghamton. His research focuses on judicial independence, selection methods, and U.S. state courts.

Suggestions for further reading

In this book
See essays 3 (Human Nature and the Constitution), 23 (Why Is My Congressional District Such a Weird Shape?), and 28 (Campaign Finance and the First Amendment).

Elsewhere
The Federalist Papers nos. 10, 65, and 68.

28

Campaign Finance and the First Amendment

Bruce Larson

Reformers and the public alike have long worried that campaign money unduly influences election outcomes and gives disproportionate clout to wealthy donors. But fixes for these concerns aren't easy. Chief among the reasons why is the Supreme Court's unease with regulations it sees as colliding with the First Amendment.

For much of American history, little regulation of campaign money existed. This changed in the 1970s, when Congress passed several bills to address rising campaign costs and the influence of donors. The most consequential of these laws, the 1974 amendments to the 1971 Federal Election Campaign Act (FECA), came in the wake of troubling Watergate-related campaign finance abuses committed by the Nixon campaign. The 1974 law created strict limits on campaign contributions and expenditures, comprehensive disclosure requirements, a new federal agency (the Federal Election Commission) to enforce the law, and a program whereby qualified presidential (although not congressional) candidates could receive public funds for their campaigns.

The legislation as passed would never be enacted, however. In a landmark ruling issued before the law took effect, the Supreme Court in *Buckley v. Valeo* (1976) invalidated the law's restrictions on campaign spending while leaving intact its limits on contributions.

The Court's analysis in *Buckley* is key to understanding roadblocks to campaign finance reform. Rejecting the government's position that equalizing influence in elections is a legitimate government aim, the Court in *Buckley* accepted only one rationale for restrictions on campaign money: the government's interest in preventing quid pro quo corruption and its appearance. Importantly, the Court felt that this corruption rationale outweighed First Amendment rights where contribution limits were concerned but not where expenditure limits were concerned. Contribution limits, it reasoned, only marginally restrict a donor's First Amendment right to express support for a candidate—support can be expressed through even modest donations—and such restrictions serve the government's aim of limiting corruption. Campaign expenditure limits, in contrast, severely hamper a spender's right to disseminate a campaign message but do little to prevent quid pro quo corruption.

The consequences of the Court's distinction were unsurprising. With no limits on spending, campaign expenditures grew sharply, limited only by what candidates could raise. By 2020, the average winning U.S. Senate candidate spent $27.2 million, and the average winning House candidate $2.4 million. With strict limits on contributions, candidates needed to raise these sums in relatively small increments: no more than $1,000 from individual donors and $5,000 from group political action committees (PACs). In 2002, Congress pegged the individual contribution limit to inflation, but even the inflation-adjusted limits ($2,800 in 2020) are low for contests costing millions of dollars. One candidate likened fundraising under FECA to "filling up a swimming pool with a tablespoon." Meanwhile, critics lamented the long hours officeholders spent fundraising at the expense of lawmaking and representation.

Independent expenditures by groups and political parties would prove especially vexing to reformers. Consistent with *Buckley*, groups were permitted to spend without limit on behalf of a candidate if (1) the expenditures were made without coordination with the candidate and (2) the spending was paid for with regulated money. This meant, for example, that a corporation could not dip into its treasury to fund independent spending. Instead, the law required the corporation to set up a PAC and finance the expenditure using strictly limited donations made voluntarily to the PAC by the company's employees.

In the 1990s, groups and political parties began circumventing these limits by using unregulated money to pay for so-called issue ads. To the average viewer, issue ads looked no different from a typical candidate ad. But because these ads stopped short of using words such as "vote for" or "vote against," they were considered *issue* advocacy rather than *election* advocacy. The distinction allowed the ads to be financed with unregulated ("soft") rather than regulated ("hard") money.

In the Bipartisan Campaign Reform Act (BCRA) in 2002, Congress sought to curb these practices by prohibiting political parties from raising soft money and banning the use of unregulated labor and corporate treasury funds for "electioneering communications"—a new category of communications designed to include candidate ads masquerading as issue ads. In a 5–4 decision, the Supreme Court upheld these provisions in *McConnell v. Federal Election Commission* (2003).

But changes in the Court's membership after *McConnell* produced a Court majority with less tolerance for regulations on group political spending. In 2010, the new majority's hostility toward regulation culminated in a landmark 5–4 case, *Citizens United v. Federal Election Commission*. Emphasizing Buckley's assertion that independent spending is by definition noncorrupting and declaring that "political speech does not lose protection 'simply because its source is a corporation,'" the Court invalidated BCRA's ban on corporate (and by extension union) treasury funds to finance independent expenditures.

The importance of the Court's ruling in *Citizens United* is difficult to overstate. Three months after the decision, the DC Circuit Court of Appeals, relying on *Citizens United*, invalidated limits on contributions to political committees that make only independent expenditures (*Speechnow.org v. FEC*, 2010). The rulings unleashed an explosion of campaign spending from so-called independent-expenditure committees (super PACs) and 501(c) social welfare groups, the latter subject to few disclosure rules. Such expenditures may now be financed by unlimited corporate and union treasury funds and by billionaires. Many of these committees have ties to the parties and candidates on whose behalf they spend.

Since the 1970s, reformers seeking tighter regulation of campaign money have confronted a Supreme Court intent on guarding the First Amendment. The Roberts Court has been particularly hostile to regulation, scuttling long-standing restrictions. The resulting surge of unregulated money in campaigns has created heightened concerns of undue influence much like those that motivated Watergate-era reformers.

About the author

Bruce Larson is a professor of political science at Gettysburg College. His teaching and research interests are in the areas of political parties, the U.S. Congress, and campaign finance.

Suggestions for further reading

In this book
See essays 22 (Who Can Vote?) and 27 (Can the Constitution Handle Political Parties?).

Elsewhere

OpenSecrets. https://www.opensecrets.org/—A nonpartisan group that makes federal and state data on money and politics available to the public.

Mutch, Robert C. 2016. *Campaign Finance: What Everyone Needs to Know.* New York: Oxford University Press.

29

Is the Administrative State Unconstitutional?

Christine Kexel Chabot

It is difficult to imagine an aspect of daily life untouched by today's administrative state. In the United States, administrative decisions govern fundamental concerns ranging from the purity of the air we breathe and the water we drink, to the safety of cars and airplanes, to student loans and mortgages, and much, much more. Given the broad reach of administrative decisions, it may come as a surprise that the U.S. Constitution does not expressly provide for the many administrative agencies that make these decisions. The Constitution establishes elected representatives such as the president and Congress, while it provides only shadowy references to other unelected actors such as principal officers and heads of departments. Does this mean that administrative agencies are unconstitutional? The answer is no, and a few key clauses of the Constitution explain why this is so.

Article II of the Constitution vests "the executive power" in a single elected president, and presidents going all the way back to George Washington have recognized that they cannot execute the laws on their own. Elected members of Congress have helped presidents by creating administrative agencies. Article I of the Constitution authorizes Congress to create agencies under its power to "make all laws which shall be Necessary and Proper for carrying into execution" the sovereign powers of the United States. Two of the very first agencies in the United States, the Departments of Foreign Affairs (later renamed State) and Treasury, were led by Thomas Jefferson and Alexander Hamilton, respectively. Executive officers at the helm of federal agencies are not elected, but pursuant to Article II, they must be appointed by an elected president and confirmed by an elected Senate. Once in office, executive officers remain accountable to the president and must comply with laws passed by Congress.

A further problem, and area of great controversy, is that laws creating agencies may delegate more power to unelected executive officers than the Constitution allows. Article I of the Constitution vests "legislative power" to "make all laws" in Congress. Absent a constitutional amendment, Congress cannot transfer its legislative power to unelected actors in another branch of government. It would surely be unconstitutional if Congress passed a law allowing executive officers to vote on bills in Congress's stead. Do extremely vague statutes create the same problem? In other words, does Congress unconstitutionally delegate legislative powers when it passes laws that allow executive officers to ban conduct that is "unfair" or not in the "public interest"? These statutory mandates are so broad that they allow unelected executive officers, and not elected members of Congress, to make almost all of the important policy decisions for a given piece of legislation. Further, officers sometimes implement these policy decisions through forward-looking and generally applicable rules that bind private parties in the same manner as legislation.

Until now, the Supreme Court has almost always rejected constitutional challenges to the scope of powers delegated by Congress, so long as the law includes an "intelligible principle" to guide the executive officer's decision. The Court has held that the vague statutes noted above satisfy this requirement, and it is difficult to imagine a law so vague that it lacks an intelligible principle. In recent years, however, critics such as Justice Gorsuch have argued that the intelligible principle requirement fails to constrain delegations of legislative power to unelected executive officers. In *Gundy v. United States* (2019), Justice Gorsuch urged the Court to reconsider this doctrine and impose a constitutional requirement that Congress decide all policy questions (or perhaps all important policy questions) in domestic statutes. Only then would Congress properly exercise its legislative power and create a sufficiently narrow law for executive officers to carry out by filling in details and finding facts.

If Justice Gorsuch's argument were adopted by a majority of the Court, it would upend long-standing precedent and invalidate scores of vague regulatory statutes. He contended that such upheaval is necessary to bring regulatory laws into line with the original meaning of the Constitution. Arguments about original meaning focus on the Constitution's text and history, and part of Justice Gorsuch's concern seemed to reflect the understanding that today we have many more administrative agencies with many more powers than agencies had at the founding.

Justice Gorsuch's historical analysis was incomplete, however, and failed to account for previously overlooked evidence that scholars have unearthed in *Gundy*'s wake. While some of the regulatory statutes approved by James Madison and other members of early Congresses were incredibly specific, other early statutes were extremely vague and allowed executive officers to resolve important policy questions. Vague statutes from the founding era might undermine Justice Gorsuch's claims about the original meaning of legislative power and Congress's ability to delegate policy questions to executive officers.

In the Court's most recent decision in *West Virginia v. EPA* (2022), Chief Justice Roberts's majority opinion reined in the Environmental Protection Agency's (EPA) policy-making authority by adopting a narrow interpretation of the Clean Air Act. In a concurrence joined by Justice Alito, Justice Gorsuch argued that the majority's narrow interpretation was required to guard against an unconstitutional delegation of legislative power. Only time will tell whether a majority of the Court will ultimately adopt Justice Gorsuch's position and hold that the Constitution requires courts to invalidate vague regulatory statutes and constrain the power exercised by executive officers who run administrative agencies.

About the author

Christine Kexel Chabot is a distinguished professor in residence at Loyola University Chicago School of Law. Her research focuses on separation of powers and agency and judicial independence.

Suggestions for further reading

In this book
See essays 13 (What Is the Purpose of the Separation of Powers?), 15 (The Crucial Power to Appoint and Remove Officials), and 16 (Who Really Makes the Laws?).

Elsewhere
Adler, Jonathan H. 2020. *Delegation and Nondelegation at the Founding.* Reason. Last modified October 16, 2020. https://reason.com/volokh/2020/10/16/delegation-and-nondelegation-at-the-founding/.

Hamburger, Philip. 2014. *Is Administrative Law Unlawful?* Chicago: University of Chicago Press.

Mashaw, Jerry. 2012. *Creating the Administrative Constitution.* New Haven, CT: Yale University Press.

McConnell, Michael. 2020. *The President Who Would Not Be King.* Princeton, NJ: Princeton University Press.

Individual Liberties

30
Does the Constitution Protect Hate Speech?

Timothy R. Johnson

While the First Amendment says "Congress shall make no law . . . abridging the freedom of speech," there are instances when the government does limit this fundamental right because allowing such speech may, directly or indirectly, infringe on another fundamental right held by United States citizens. Consider *hate speech*, which arises from "hostile, discriminatory, and prejudicial attitudes toward another person's innate characteristics: sex, race, ethnicity, religion, or sexual orientation." Even such mean-spirited speech seems to enjoy protection under the absolute wording of the free speech clause. The problem is that if the government protects such hate-filled speech, it likely infringes on another right held by those to whom the speech is aimed—their equal protection right found in the Fourteenth Amendment. Thus, the ultimate arbiter of which right prevails, the U.S. Supreme Court, faces the dilemma of protecting one fundamental right over another. Therefore, deciding such cases is so difficult.

Consider the first time the Court ruled on a case that touched on hate speech—*Chaplinsky v. New Hampshire* (1942). Walter Chaplinsky, a Jehovah's Witness, was distributing literature that criticized other religious practices. While on a public sidewalk in the city of Rochester, New Hampshire, he allegedly used hate-filled speech, including saying to a police officer, "You are a God damned 'racketeer' and 'a damned Fascist' and the whole government of Rochester are Fascists or agents of Fascists." For this behavior, Chaplinsky was arrested under a state law that prohibited offensive and annoying speech aimed at other people in a public place. When he appealed his case to the Supreme Court, the justices unanimously ruled that there are certain exceptions to the First Amendment's protections, depending on the category of speech. For example, obscenities, certain types of slander and profanity, and "fighting words" are not protected.

Chaplinsky begs the question, If speech is meant to harm a person to whom it is aimed, does this mean it is not protected under the First Amendment? More recently, the Court took up this question in *Snyder v. Phelps* (2011) after Frank Phelps and his followers from the Westboro Baptist Church protested the funeral of Marine Lance Corporal Matthew Snyder. Neither Phelps nor his followers directly interfered with the funeral proceedings, but they stood along the funeral route and displayed signs that said things like "God Hates the USA / Thank God for 9/11," "Thank God for Dead Soldiers," and "Don't Pray for the USA." Snyder filed a civil suit claiming the protest was hateful and caused him (and his family) emotional distress. The Court ruled that because Phelps's speech related to issues of public interest and occurred on public property, it was entitled to special protection under the First Amendment.

Phelps was not the first time the Court protected what some might consider hate speech. In *R.A.V. v. City of St. Paul, Minnesota* (1992), a group of teenagers targeted a Black family by burning a cross in their yard. The boys were found guilty of violating St. Paul, Minnesota's Motivated Crime Ordinance, which prohibited "the placement of objects or graffiti on public or private property that the person knows will arouse alarm or anger in others based on race, color, creed, religion, or gender." R.A.V.'s attorney argued the ordinance was impermissibly content based because it included specific categories of speech that may cause anger. The Supreme Court found the ordinance unconstitutional because it prohibited otherwise permitted speech, simply based on the subjects the speech addressed.

Although hate speech might stem from subjects such as race, religion, and gender, a government cannot pick and choose which subjects an individual might address with "fighting words." For example, under St. Paul's ordinance, if an individual aroused alarm or anger after speaking ill of a person based on one of these traits, there may be no punishment because the city self-selected unfavorable subjects for its ordinance.

Further, just because speech may seem to be hateful does not automatically mean it can (or will) be regulated. Recently, the Court issued a unanimous decision in *Matal v. Tam* (2017). In this case, the justices argued, "Speech that demeans on the basis of race, ethnicity, gender, religion, age, disability, or any other similar ground is hateful; but the proudest boast of our free speech jurisprudence is that we protect the freedom to express 'the thought that we hate.'"

In the end, the government (and usually the Supreme Court) tries to protect people from being treated in a hateful manner, even if doing so will harm another person's freedom of speech. That said, while hate speech can be regulated and punished, the Court usually errs on the side of protecting speech no matter how hurtful it may seem—including protecting cross burning in certain instances (*Virginia v. Black* [2003]).

About the author

Timothy R. Johnson is Horace T. Morse Distinguished Professor of Political Science and Law at the University of Minnesota. His research focuses on Supreme Court decision-making and oral arguments.

Suggestions for further reading

In this book
See essays 1 (Why Do We Have a Constitution?), 31 (Does the Constitution Protect the Right to Lie?), and 32 (Can I Be Prosecuted for Telling Someone to Break the Law?).

Elsewhere
Wisconsin v. Mitchell, 508 U.S. 476 (1993).

Virginia v. Black, 538 U.S. 343 (2003).

31
Does the Constitution Protect the Right to Lie?

Keith J. Bybee

Is there a constitutional right to lie? One answer to this question is no. Another answer to this question is yes. Both answers are correct.

To see how these contradictory answers can both be right, consider that one of the central aims of the constitutional protection of free speech is to promote wide-ranging discussion in public affairs. Why is this an important goal? According to the Supreme Court, we have to begin with the understanding that different opinions often possess at least a grain of truth. To make progress toward the whole truth, conflicting opinions must be pitted against one another in open debate. As Justice Oliver Wendell Holmes wrote over a century ago, "The best test of truth is the power of the thought to get itself accepted in the competition of the market." By attending to the freewheeling opinions of fervent dissenters and impassioned partisans, the public identifies error, learns new truths, and gains a more vital grasp of the truths it already knows to be sound. It is through free expression and vigorous argument that people identify the information necessary to govern themselves. "This is," Holmes argued, "the theory of our Constitution."

But not everything said, published, or posted is of equal constitutional importance. The Supreme Court has identified various forms of expression—including obscenity, commercial advertising, and fighting words—that do not make essential contributions to the pursuit of truth in the all-important free marketplace of ideas. Such forms of "low-value speech" do not receive heightened constitutional protection, and they can be readily censored.

The Court considers false statements of fact to be low-value speech. This does not mean that false factual statements are never of any use at all. For example, members of the Court have observed that lies are helpful for providing the sick with comfort (something to remember if a Supreme

Court justice ever visits you in the hospital). However, unlike the core speech that comprises public debate, lies do not advance the truth-seeking goals served by the free exchange of ideas. As a result, the Court has often allowed lies to be prohibited by the government. As Justice Alito noted in *United States v. Alvarez* (2012), "Time and again this Court has recognized that as a general matter false factual statements possess no intrinsic First Amendment value. All told, there are more than 100 federal criminal statutes that punish false statements made in connection with areas of federal agency concern." Thus, there is no formal constitutional right to lie.

Yet at the same time, the Constitution often safeguards lying. Why? Because while false statements of fact themselves have little First Amendment value, they are nonetheless inextricably bound up with the free expression that the First Amendment protects. As the Court noted in *New York Times v. Sullivan* (1964), debate in the free marketplace of ideas is meant to be "uninhibited, robust, and wide-open." In such debate, vehement attacks, caustic criticism, and outright lies are inevitable. Can't the government police and purify the free marketplace of ideas by penalizing low-value speech whenever it crops up? Here the Court has responded with a resounding no, reasoning that official efforts to prohibit lying can fatally undermine the great goals of free expression.

The problem is one of self-censorship. A law requiring speakers to guarantee the truth of their statements would lead many to refuse to participate in public debate for fear that they might be punished for misstating a fact. Lies do not positively facilitate the functioning of the free marketplace of ideas and may wreak havoc in public affairs. Yet the attempt to ban lying can chill the exercise of free speech, imposing a solution that is far more harmful than the problem the government seeks to solve. Thus, whenever requirements of truthfulness would threaten to suppress valuable expression, the Constitution protects the right to lie.

About the author

Keith J. Bybee is a professor of law and political science at Syracuse University. His more recent research examines the relationship between law and civility.

Suggestions for further reading

In this book
See essays 30 (Does the Constitution Protect Hate Speech?) and 51 (Taking the Fifth).

Elsewhere

Bybee, Keith J., and Laura Jenkins. 2020. "Free Speech, Free Press and Fake News: What If the Marketplace of Ideas Isn't about Identifying the Truth?" In *Free Speech Theory: Understanding the Controversies*, edited by Helen J. Knowles and Brandon T. Metroka, 97–120. New York: Peter Lang.

Smolla, Rodney A. 1992. *Free Speech in an Open Society*. New York: Knopf.

32

Can I Be Prosecuted for Telling Someone to Break the Law?

David E. Klein

> Congress shall make no law . . . abridging the freedom of speech.
> —U.S. Constitution, First Amendment

Perhaps the best place to start any analysis of a free speech claim is with a reminder that the First Amendment is not concerned with ordinary, unobjectionable speech. We don't need protection from the government when we say things most other people agree with or find innocuous. So unless we take the clause to be empty words with no practical effect, we must understand it to provide some protection when we communicate things that other people—especially those in power—find wrong, offensive, and even dangerous.

There are three powerful insights behind this protection. The most fundamental is that a society cannot improve, or even remain healthy, if it is not open to criticism and new ideas. The second is that government officials will always feel some temptation to use the power of government to limit speech. They have an interest in limiting criticism of themselves as well as of existing policies and institutions, they may sincerely believe that some opponents are dangerous, and constituents will often pressure them to crack down on speech that the constituents don't like. Finally, many people will self-censor in the face of threats of prosecution, limiting the circulation of criticisms and innovative ideas. The First Amendment aims to promote open and fruitful public debate by making it harder for government to narrow its scope directly or through threats.

It is precisely when we feel most passionately that something is wrong with the status quo that we're most likely to use inflammatory rhetoric. Consider the kinds of language you might expect to use or hear around you if you participate in a "Right to Life" or "Black Lives Matter" rally.

Or think of some expressions you or your friends might use in a heated discussion of politics. Now imagine that it was easy for the government to convict and incarcerate people for urging others to break the law. Anyone saying something like "No justice, no peace," "We'll do whatever it takes," or "Anyone who votes for that should be shot!" would be at grave risk. As a result, we would have far less of the free exchange of views that is essential to a democracy.

It appears, then, that the answer to the title question must sometimes be no. The First Amendment commits us to allowing, in at least some situations, speech that we might see as inciting lawbreaking or even violence.

This does not mean that we must tolerate all speech, no matter how risky. As Justice Holmes famously wrote in the 1919 case *Schenck v. U.S.*, the "most stringent protection of free speech would not protect a man in falsely shouting fire in a theatre and causing a panic." Or to take an example that's both cruder and more directly relevant to this essay, imagine a crime boss who orders his underlings to burn down a theater that refused to pay for "protection." Would we take seriously the boss's argument that he cannot be held responsible for the arson because his activity was limited to speech? Speech directing employees to commit violent crimes tears at the fabric of society without any potential compensating benefits. Most people would readily agree that it can be prosecuted without violating the spirit and aims of the First Amendment.

The challenge, then, is to decide *how much* protection to give to speech that could have harmful effects. As a society, we have struggled to come to an answer, often approving reduced protections when threats like the Cold War and terrorism have loomed large. The Supreme Court showed evidence of the same struggle well into the twentieth century. The justices were unable to settle on a single test, and regardless of whether the test used was or wasn't very protective in theory, the Court frequently upheld convictions of communists or socialists. For instance, in *Schenck* itself, the Court unanimously upheld a conviction for advocating resistance to the draft during World War I.

In 1969, however, the Court adopted an approach that is highly protective of speech. *Brandenburg v. Ohio* involved the conviction of a Ku Klux Klan leader for advocating violence and lawbreaking. Although the justices undoubtedly found the Klan's language to be repulsive and even dangerous, they voted unanimously to overturn the conviction, on the ground that the danger was not immediate enough to justify prosecution. The Court held that government may not "proscribe advocacy of the use of force or of law violation except where such advocacy is directed to inciting or producing imminent lawless action and is likely to incite or produce such action."

The importance of the words "imminent" and "likely" can be illustrated with an example. Imagine a union leader who becomes worked up while addressing striking workers and yells, "If they won't talk seriously, we'll burn the plant down!" That isolated shout would not justify a conviction under the *Brandenburg* test: we don't have good reason to believe the leader was trying to produce an act of arson in that moment or, even if he was, that his words had much chance of inducing the strikers to act. In contrast, the *Brandenburg* test might not stand in the way of a prosecution if the union leader spoke at length about the benefits of attacking the plant, pointed out flammable materials in the vicinity, and ended with "Show them what we're willing to do right now, or they'll never take us seriously!"

Under the *Brandenburg* test, even intemperate and inflammatory speech receives considerable protection. As of today, the test appears to be respected and well established. However, it is doubtful that the crucial question underlying it—how we should weigh the risks of dangerous speech against the risk of having too little speech—can ever be conclusively settled.

About the author

David E. Klein is a professor of political science at Eastern Michigan University. His work focuses primarily on judicial decision-making and the development of the law.

Suggestions for further reading

In this book
See essays 30 (Does the Constitution Protect Hate Speech?) and 31 (Does the Constitution Protect the Right to Lie?).

Elsewhere
Abrams v. United States, 250 U.S. 616 (1919).

Brandenburg v. Ohio, 395 U.S. 444 (1969).

33
Do the Media Have Special Rights?

Mark J. Richards

The First Amendment states, "Congress shall make no law . . . abridging the freedom of speech, or of the press." Does the specific mention of the press imply that the media have distinct rights as compared to other speakers? As the fourth estate, a check on government, do the media have special rights? With broadcast media, cable carriers and internet providers serving roles in promoting freedom of expression, what special obligations do these types of media have?

The principle of content neutrality lies at the foundation of the Supreme Court's free expression jurisprudence. When the government targets the content or viewpoint of expression, the justices apply the strict scrutiny standard to such a content-based law. Strict scrutiny means the law must be the least restrictive means of achieving a compelling interest, a difficult standard for the government to meet, and the justices are likely to strike down any law that targets the content of expression. Most forms of media regulation are judged by the strict scrutiny standard. Even newer forms of media such as the internet and video games are protected by strict scrutiny. When California attempted to carve out an exception to the First Amendment in order to single out video games for stricter regulation than movies or television, the Court rejected the attempt and reaffirmed the presumption in favor of freedom for new forms of media. Although media don't have special rights, media rights are generally protected as highly as the rights of any other speaker.

When the government regulates the time, place, or manner of expression in a content-neutral way, and when the government regulates conduct rather than expression, the justices apply the intermediate scrutiny standard, which makes it a bit easier for the government to defend a content-neutral law, as the law must be necessary to achieve an important government interest. One example of a regulation of conduct is that when people have information about a crime, they are required to testify when called before a grand jury. When that person is a newspaper reporter, requiring the reporter to testify could compromise a confidential source. The Supreme Court, however, declined to establish a First Amendment privilege for reporters to be exempt from grand jury testimony requirements. Some states have passed statutes known as media shield laws to establish such a privilege to protect media, but such a privilege is not required by the First Amendment.

Regulations of broadcast media, television and radio stations that are delivered over the air, are an exception to the principle of content neutrality. Regulations of broadcast media are treated according to intermediate scrutiny because the scarcity of the broadcast spectrum requires government licensing and the need to balance the public's right to receive information. By contrast, the Court has judged regulations of the internet according to strict scrutiny because the internet is different from broadcast media. The internet is vast, democratic in the sense that anyone can start a website or express themselves on the internet, and there's no need for licensing of a scarce spectrum. Like video games, the internet has been afforded the presumption of freedom established by the principle of content neutrality.

Through Section 230 of the Communications Decency Act, internet service providers and other online hosts of third-party content (e.g., Twitter, Facebook, and YouTube) cannot be held liable for the expression of third parties, with some exceptions. With the rise of disinformation and hate speech that incites violence, critics have called for a revision of Section 230, while social media platforms have become more active in censoring such expression. Given the speed at which social media content can go viral and considering that social media giants have considerable latitude to censor, regulation of expression on social media is moving beyond the ability of government to act in a precise and timely way.

If the government were to require a bookstore to carry a certain book, or a movie theater to show a particular film, the First Amendment would be violated. However, what if the federal government required cable television providers to carry local broadcast stations? The Court ruled that such "must-carry" rules did not run afoul of the First Amendment because the rules enhanced freedom of expression by ensuring that cable subscribers had access to valuable local news, public affairs, and sports programming. Like Section 230, such rules are seen as enhancing freedom of expression.

Although media do not have special rights, the principle of content neutrality establishes a strong presumption in favor of freedom and against the regulation of various forms of media. Evolving forms of media will continue to test the strength of the First Amendment freedom of expression.

About the author

Mark J. Richards is a professor in the Grand Valley State University Department of Political Science. His research examines U.S. Supreme Court decision-making as well as freedom of expression in international and comparative law.

Suggestions for further reading

In this book
See essays 30 (Does the Constitution Protect Hate Speech?), 31 (Does the Constitution Protect the Right to Lie?), and 32 (Can I Be Prosecuted for Telling Someone to Break the Law?).

Elsewhere
Richards, Mark J. 2013. *The Politics of Freedom of Expression: The Decisions of the Supreme Court of the United States.* New York: Palgrave Macmillan.

Bollinger, Lee C. 2010. *Uninhibited, Robust, and Wide-Open: A Free Press for a New Century.* New York: Oxford University Press.

Epps, Garrett, ed. 2008. *Freedom of the Press: The First Amendment; Its Constitutional History and the Contemporary Debate.* Buffalo: Prometheus Books.

34

Is All Religious Behavior Protected?

Barry Pyle

> Congress shall make no law . . . prohibiting the free exercise
> (of religion).
>
> —U.S. Constitution, First Amendment

The free exercise clause of the First Amendment expresses the importance the U.S. founders placed on religious freedom. But how extensive
is this freedom, and what does it encompass? For many years, the Supreme
Court has recognized a distinction between what people believe and what
they do. As the Court said in *Reynolds v. U.S.* (1878), "Laws are made
for the government of actions, and while they cannot interfere with mere
religious belief and opinions, they may with practices." This distinction
between belief and practice raises a crucial question: When, if ever, do
religious practices merit special protection compared to similar behavior
with secular motivations?

In *Reynolds*, the Court declined to give religious practices special
protection. In its view, George Reynolds's religious beliefs gave him no
special claim to be a polygamist compared to someone with a secular
desire to have multiple spouses. This did not mean the Court was generally
unsympathetic to religious exercise claims. In another landmark case,
Cantwell v. Connecticut (1940), the Court overturned the convictions of
Jehovah's Witnesses, who were prosecuted for soliciting donations without
prior approval and for playing records (with permission) that some lis-
teners found offensive. In affirming the Witnesses' freedom of action, the
Court gave particular emphasis to people's right to share their views and
beliefs with others.

Throughout the 1940s through the 1950s, the Court gave elevated protection to the communication of religious beliefs but otherwise provided

few protections for religious behavior. As late as 1961, in *Braunfeld v. Brown*, the Court upheld a Pennsylvania law requiring businesses to be closed on Sundays. Orthodox Jewish business owners, whose religion forbade them to do business on Saturdays, argued that the Sunday closing put them at a serious disadvantage for following the dictates of their religion. The *Braunfeld* Court reasoned that the state possessed an interest in a common day of rest and that any resulting economic hardships only indirectly burdened religion.

The Court changed course soon after, most notably in *Sherbert v. Verner* (1963) and *Yoder v. Wisconsin* (1972). In *Sherbert*, it sided with an employee who was fired for not working on her Sabbath and denied unemployment benefits. *Yoder* applied the logic of *Sherbert* and allowed Old Order Amish parents to remove their children from school after the eighth grade for religious reasons. Together, these cases created the *Sherbert/Yoder* test, which necessitated a compelling interest when the state sought to regulate actions in ways that substantially infringed on religious practice.

Demanding a compelling interest kept the protection of religious liberty on a level similar to that of political speech. Still, the Court's shift did not mean that the state always lost free exercise cases. Between 1972 and 1990, the Court decided that the state either did not substantially infringe on religion or had a sufficient interest in creating the social security system, esprit de corps in the military, security in prison, or a tax system. In fact, the only cases where the Court consistently supported religious individuals involved state denials of unemployment benefits after someone was fired for religious observances. And in *Employment Division v. Smith* (1990), the Court largely abandoned the *Sherbert/Yoder* test.

Smith involved the use of an illegal drug, peyote, in Native American religious ceremonies. Writing for the majority, Justice Antonin Scalia posited that granting a religious exemption in this case would require exempting people from all civic obligations that run counter to religious belief. The Court held that as long as legal restrictions apply to nonreligious and religious behavior equally and are not intended to interfere with religion, governments are free to enforce those restrictions even when they do interfere with religious practice.

Restrictions of religious practice can still be found unconstitutional after *Smith*. Under its conception of strict neutrality, religious liberty and actions must have the same protection as secular liberty and actions. Just a few years later, *Lukumi v. City of Hialeah* (1993) struck down a law banning ritual animal sacrifice because the law violated neutrality by targeting a religion.

Nevertheless, the main effect of *Smith* was to give religious practices less protection. The decision was widely criticized, and in 1993, Congress passed the Religious Freedom Restoration Act (RFRA) in an attempt to restore the *Sherbert/Yoder* test and its elevated protection of religious practice. The attempt was only partially successful. In *Boerne v. Flores* (1997), the Court responded by telling Congress that while it may hold its own statutes to the more exacting standard, it may not hold the Court or states to the *Sherbert/Yoder* standard through mere legislation.

Under *Smith* and RFRA, if a case involves the national government or a state with its own RFRA, the Court applies a statutory version of the *Sherbert/Yoder* test (see *Burwell v. Hobby Lobby* [2014]). If a state does not have a state-based RFRA, the Court applies *Smith* and *Lukumi*. For example, *Trinity Lutheran Church v. Comer* (2017) found that a state treated religion in a nonneutral fashion when it disqualified a religious day care but not secular ones from receiving a government benefit.

Recently, tensions between religious free exercise and sexual orientation and gender identification antidiscrimination laws have heightened attention to the Court's definition of religious liberty and neutrality. *Masterpiece Cakeshop v. Colorado Civil Rights Commission* (2018) demanded that states avoid impermissible hostile treatment of religious individuals who deny services to same-sex couples. *Fulton v. City of Philadelphia* (2021) mandated that governments must equally apply all program rules regardless of a participant's religious views concerning same-sex and unmarried couples as foster parents. *Fulton* also represented the first time that a majority of justices may be willing to replace the *Reynolds* neutrality of *Smith* and *Lukumi* with a return to the elevated notion of neutrality or the special protection consistent with the *Sherbert/Yoder* test.

About the author

Barry Pyle is a professor of political science, prelaw advisor, and coach of the Mock Trial and Moot Court teams at Eastern Michigan University. His research interests focus on judicial diversity in state and federal appellate courts as well as decision-/policy-making on the U.S. Supreme Court.

Suggestions for further reading

In this book
See essays 35 (What Does "Separation of Church and State" Mean?), 45 (Regulating Private Discrimination), and 47 (Is There a Right to Same-Sex Marriage?).

Elsewhere
Employment Division v. Smith, 494 U.S. 872 (1990).

City of Boerne v. Flores, 521 U.S. 507 (1997).

Masterpiece Cakeshop v. Colorado Civil Rights Commission, 138 S. Ct. 1719 (2018).

35
What Does "Separation of Church and State" Mean?

Chris Kromphardt

> Congress shall make no law respecting an establishment of religion.
>
> —U.S. Constitution, First Amendment

The stakes for the question of what separation of church and state means are high. These stakes are to be expected, given that the profound debates over what the Constitution requires, permits, and prohibits in this area of civil liberties are some of the most heated in American politics.

These debates have extended into the chambers of the U.S. Supreme Court. The views of these nine justices are the most important for determining what separation of church and state means. When it comes to the implications of the establishment clause, the first ten words of the First Amendment, most justices can be easily classified as holding either *separationist* or *accommodationist* views.

In the strongest separationist form, the separation of church and state evoked by the establishment clause means that no level of government, from the federal to the local, can require citizens to hold a particular set of religious beliefs, nor is it permitted to show active or symbolic support to any institution devoted to furthering those beliefs. The countervailing accommodationist perspective maintains that while government officials are prohibited from wielding the force of law to coerce people in order to support favored religious beliefs, they are otherwise permitted to show support for some religions over others.

There are some exceptions to this classification. Some justices hold altogether idiosyncratic views of the establishment clause—for example, in *Elk Grove Unified School District v. Newdow*, Clarence Thomas expressed skepticism about the clause's selective incorporation, arguing that it cannot be held to limit actions taken by any of the fifty states.

Among generally separationist justices, there is disagreement about the role of tradition—for example, in the case of *Town of Greece v. Galloway*, Elena Kagan sided with accommodationist justices on the constitutionality of prayer to open government meetings because of the long history of the practice. Among accommodationist justices, there is a heated debate over whether social pressure, such as that faced by public schoolchildren to conform to others, rises to the level of coercion. In *Lee v. Weisman*, normally accommodationist Justice Anthony Kennedy wrote for a majority consisting mostly of separationist justices that social pressure could be coercive, a position his fellow accommodationist Justice Antonin Scalia vigorously disagreed with in dissent.

Establishment cases arise from a variety of facts. Because establishment is a civil liberty, there is the requirement of state action: a representative of the government must have acted in a way that plausibly raises an establishment claim. Famous cases have involved numerous forms of state action, including erecting symbols with religious associations—such as the Ten Commandments, a Jewish menorah, or a Christian crèche—or providing funding for school-related expenses, such as the provision of textbooks or reimbursement for travel to and from campus, that benefit religious educational institutions.

Historically, there have been Supreme Court cases where majorities supported the separationist account of the establishment clause. The justices who wrote these opinions held skeptical views of substantial overlap between church and state. To them, government and religious institutions function best when largely independent of each other.

Today, it is apparent that a majority of justices do not hold these skeptical views. The constitutional text is ambiguous, so accommodationist justices have no trouble reaching different outcomes when cases concern subtly different facts. When Supreme Court personnel changes, the meaning of the separation of church and state can also change. This effect is clear when one considers government displays that include religious symbols. Whereas, for example, a previous Court majority had struck down a government display depicting the birth of Jesus Christ, a new Court majority ruled in 2019 that a forty-foot cross, a symbol of Jesus's death and resurrection, on public land was permissible.

As mentioned above, it is the views of the nine justices that matter most in determining what separation of church and state means. However, members of the judicial branch are not the only ones who have a say.

Practically speaking, this meaning also depends on the enforcement of the judicial outcome, which can be far removed from the hands of the justices in the majority. Nowhere is this enforcement dilemma clearer than in the area of public school prayer, which implicates the establishment clause. In 1962, in *Engel v. Vitale*, the Supreme Court took an unambiguous, separationist position against the daily recitation by schoolchildren of a prayer written by the state board of regents. However, the Supreme Court obviously is ill-equipped to enforce this opinion—it prompts a chuckle to picture a black-robed justice sitting in a classroom, awaiting the faintest whisper of a constitutional violation. Indeed, public school prayer persists to the present: in 2019, 12 percent of teenagers in the South reportedly had had a public school teacher lead their class in prayer.

This discussion raises the question, Will the meaning of separation of church and state ever become fixed? It is of course possible to amend the Constitution to resolve the ambiguity of the establishment clause, but this is unlikely to happen. How the establishment clause is interpreted will continue to depend a lot on what the nine justices perceive it to require, permit, and prohibit. Over just a few decades, the Court has swung hard from a separationist majority to an accommodationist one. While in the near future, the Court is likely to continue this trend, further down the road, a new Court might decide to erect a less permeable wall separating church and state.

About the author

Chris Kromphardt is an education support services manager at the Public Policy Center at the University of Iowa. His research addresses judicial decision-making and the determinants of attitudes toward judicial institutions.

Suggestions for further reading

In this book
See essays 1 (Why Do We Have a Constitution?) and 34 (Is All Religious Behavior Protected?).

Elsewhere
Epstein, Lee, and Eric Posner. 2022. "The Roberts Court and the Transformation of Constitutional Protections for Religion: A Statistical Portrait." *Supreme Court Review* 2021 (1): 315–47.

Gillman, Howard, and Erwin Chemerinsky. 2020. *The Religion Clauses.* New York: Oxford University Press.

Pew Research Center. 2019. "For a Lot of American Teens, Religion Is a Regular Part of the Public School Day." Last modified October 3, 2019. https://www.pewforum.org/2019/10/03/for-a-lot-of-american-teens -religion-is-a-regular-part-of-the-public-school-day/.

36
Does a Twitter Ban
Violate the Constitution?

Lawrence Baum

In January 2021, Twitter announced that it would prevent President Donald Trump from using its service in the future, closing a Twitter account that had served as a key communication vehicle for the president. Other platforms such as Facebook and YouTube took similar actions around the same time.

Mr. Trump and some of his supporters denounced these actions as a violation of his right to free speech. If they were referring to freedom of speech as a general concept, they may or may not have been right. But if they were arguing that Twitter's actions violated the president's right to free speech under the U.S. Constitution, they probably were wrong.

The reason is simple: the Constitution's protections of free speech are protections only against governments and their personnel. The First Amendment (and the Bill of Rights as a whole) begins "Congress shall make no law." The Fourteenth Amendment begins "No state shall." Nowhere in the Constitution are private institutions prohibited from limiting speech. Indeed, with the exception of the Thirteenth Amendment's prohibition of slavery, which the Supreme Court has interpreted to prohibit some forms of racial discrimination, the Constitution does not protect any rights against violations in the private sector. After the Fourteenth Amendment became part of the Constitution in 1868, some people argued that the term "state" encompassed private parties within a state. But the Supreme Court rejected that argument, and it has adhered to that rejection.

Clear as this principle is, it is often overlooked. That is understandable because of the broad conception of legal rights that pervades the United States. If a company fires employees because of their political activities or refuses to hire women, our natural reaction is that the company must have violated the Constitution. But it has not.

This does not mean that there are no protections of rights in the private sector. Congress and state legislatures have substantial power to prohibit such violations by enacting statutes. Congress has used this power a good deal to prohibit discrimination by private institutions. Refusal to hire someone because of race or sex, for instance, violates Title VII of the Civil Rights Act of 1964. Presidents and governors also have some power to protect rights in the private sector, and they too have made use of this power to prohibit discrimination. But the legislative and executive branches of government have not been nearly as active in protecting rights other than equality, so these other rights, including free speech, have limited legal support in the private sector.

All this means that the line between government and the private sector is quite consequential. But this line is not always clear. Government and private institutions are often intertwined: many companies and private universities receive substantial sums of money from the government and assist it in carrying out its policies, and their activities may be heavily regulated by government agencies. Does that intertwining make them governmental for purposes of the Constitution?

The Supreme Court's answer is mostly "no," and that has been especially true since the 1970s. As a general rule, action by a private institution is treated as governmental only if a government actually participated in that action, no matter how close the ties between the institution and government are. In *Rendell-Baker v. Kohn* (1982), nearly all the students at a private school had been referred to it by state and local agencies, the school received more than 90 percent of its budget from governments, and it was required to comply with many state regulations in order to receive government funding. But the Court said that the school's firing of teachers could not be challenged as a violation of their constitutional rights because the government did not take part in the firing itself. Under the same principle, professional sports leagues whose teams receive massive public subsidies do not violate constitutional rights when they fine players and coaches for criticizing umpires or referees.

Mr. Trump has sued Twitter for violation of his First Amendment rights. He argues that Twitter's actions were heavily influenced by pressure from Democratic government officials, so that the companies and those officials were working in concert. This argument reflects a recognition that the First Amendment does not apply to private companies that act on their own.

Some Republicans in Congress have proposed new regulations of Twitter and other social media that excluded President Trump. Such regulations could be challenged under the First Amendment, because they were adopted by the government. But unless the Supreme Court changes its current legal doctrines, Twitter's own actions cannot be challenged on constitutional grounds. And with few exceptions, the same is true of other actions by nongovernmental institutions. Thus the Constitution's broad protections of rights have a fundamental and consequential limitation.

About the author

Lawrence Baum is a professor emeritus of political science at Ohio State University. The primary focus of his research is judicial decision-making.

Suggestions for further reading

In this book
See essays 28 (Campaign Finance and the First Amendment) and 45 (Regulating Private Discrimination).

Elsewhere
Rendell-Baker v. Kohn, 457 U.S. 830 (1982).

Manhattan Community Access Corp. v. Halleck, 139 S. Ct. 1921 (2019).

37

Does the Second Amendment Give Me the Right to Carry a Gun?

William Merkel

> A well regulated Militia, being necessary to the security of a free State, the right of the people to keep and bear Arms, shall not be infringed.
>
> —U.S. Constitution, Second Amendment

What is the point of the Second Amendment? Virtually everyone agrees that its language, ratified in 1791, reflected a long-standing Anglo-American suspicion of standing armies and a preference for citizen militias over expensive military establishments, which were associated with corruption, profiteering, excessive borrowing and spending, and the temptation to pursue ill-advised military adventures. But militias have faded in importance, leaving us with the much more difficult and divisive question of what, if any, purpose the Second Amendment has in contemporary society.

The framing generation's assumptions concerning societal commitment to mandatory militia service were not consonant with reality for very long: in the years after the War of 1812, the system of compulsory militia duty familiar to colonial British America and the Revolutionary generation faded from view. Thus, universal manhood gun ownership as a concomitant to compulsory militia duty lost its relevance. At the same time, many Americans, particularly in the West and South, came to associate gun ownership with self-reliance and individualism, and the "gun culture" that remains pronounced in those regions to this day likely traces its roots to this period.

After the Civil War, Confederate sympathizers made disarmament of African Americans, including Union Army veterans, a priority as they sought to reestablish white supremacist domination in the South. "Black codes" in states such as South Carolina made it a criminal offense under state law for African Americans to possess firearms. Supporters of Reconstruction, particularly Radical Republicans in the Thirty-Ninth Congress, designed the Fourteenth Amendment to provide a permanent constitutional basis for African American civil equality and to nullify the black codes and other measures that aimed at perpetuating the subordination of African Americans in the South. In 1866, leading sponsors of the amendment in Congress, including Senator Jacob Howard and Representative John Bingham, suggested that the Fourteenth Amendment would make the Bill of Rights binding on state governments in the same manner that the Bill of Rights guarantees already bound the national government. In this context, Howard and Bingham spoke of the Second Amendment in a manner that implied a private right to armed self-defense as much as it did a civil right to service in the lawfully established militia on equal terms with whites.

The Supreme Court's first Second Amendment case, *United States v. Cruikshank* (1876), addressed the notorious Colfax massacre of 1873. The Court overturned convictions of three persons charged by federal authorities with violating the civil rights of more than one hundred African Americans killed while assembling with arms to protest a contested election. The Court reasoned that the Second Amendment did not protect anyone against abuses by private actors or persons acting under state as opposed to federal governmental authority. The Supreme Court next took up the Second Amendment in *Presser v. Illinois* (1886), holding that it did not protect a right to organize a private, armed militia unlicensed by state authority and that the amendment did not apply in any context against state as opposed to federal action.

The Supreme Court finally turned to the substantive scope of the constitutional right to arms in *United States v. Miller* in 1939, holding that the application of the National Firearms Act to prosecute two gangsters for transporting sawed-off shotguns across state lines did not implicate the Second Amendment, as the weapons in question were not suitable for use in militia service. For the better part of two centuries, then, what little judicial construction of the Second Amendment there was appeared consistent with academic opinion on the subject, which read the constitutional right to arms as focused on the lawfully established state militia and weapons suitable for use therein.

Things changed decidedly with *District of Columbia v. Heller* (2008), in which Justice Scalia, writing for a 5–4 Court, relied on the Second

Amendment to invalidate DC laws, making it all but impossible to keep an operational handgun in the home for purposes of self-defense. *Heller* is a pointedly originalist decision, and Justice Scalia placed great weight on founding-era sources to support his conclusion that the militia-focused language in the Second Amendment was merely a preface that did not limit the scope of what he termed the operational clause protecting the right to keep and bear arms. For Justice Scalia, that right was understood at the time of ratification to mean a right to have commonly used weapons for lawful purposes, notably including self-defense.

Academic historians who specialize in the political thought of the founding era have expressed considerable disagreement with Justice Scalia's reading. For instance, they point to the debates in the House of Representatives on the proposed Second Amendment. The debate records include the comments of twelve members, each of whom discussed militia-focused concerns, such as conscientious objection to military service, but none of whom mentioned the use of firearms for individual self-defense or hunting game. Nevertheless, *Heller* has resonated with supporters of gun rights, including a majority of justices on the Supreme Court. In *McDonald v. City of Chicago* (2010), a 5–4 Court held that the right recognized in *Heller* applied against all governments in the United States, not just the federal government and DC.

Today, therefore, any regulation of guns may be struck down for excessive interference with a right to self-defense. What that will mean in practice is still an open question. In *Heller*, Justice Scalia wrote that nothing in his opinion should be read to call into question the permissibility of long-standing prohibitions on uncommon or particularly dangerous weapons, on weapons possession by felons or the mentally ill, or on carrying guns in sensitive places, such as government buildings or schools. Nevertheless, those prohibitions—like all others—are now open to challenge. What prohibitions and regulations are allowed will depend on the courts' views of the scope of the individual right to self-defense and the validity of society's reasons for placing limits on its exercise.

About the author

William Merkel is an associate professor at the Charleston School of Law and holds advanced degrees in history as well as law. His work focuses on constitutional law and history and on international law.

Suggestions for further reading

In this book
See essays 6 (How Can We Tell What the Constitution Means?) and 8 (What Can States Do?).

Elsewhere

Cornell, Saul. 2008. *A Well-Regulated Militia: The Founding Fathers and the Origins of Gun Control in America*. New York: Oxford University Press.

Halbrook, Stephen P. 2019. *The Founders' Second Amendment*. Lanham, MD: Rowman and Littlefield.

Winkler, Adam. 2011. *Gunfight: The Battle over the Right to Bear Arms in America*. New York: W. W. Norton.

38

The Takings Clause

Robert Howard

Nor shall [any person] be deprived of life, liberty, or property, without due process of law; nor shall private property be taken for public use without just compensation.

—U.S. Constitution, Fifth Amendment takings clause

Although private property is considered nearly sacred by many people in the United States, the Constitution contains surprisingly few ways to protect it. For a time, owners who objected to government actions could reasonably hope to prevail in suits brought under the Constitution's contract clause or the judicially created "liberty of contract" doctrine of the Fourteenth Amendment. But the contract clause is now understood to have a limited scope, and the Court has abandoned the liberty of contract doctrine. Property rights advocates today look to the takings clause of the Fifth Amendment.

Governments traditionally have the power of *eminent domain*, the power to take private property for public use. Governments need this power to accomplish public goals. Usually, this means taking land to create a road, a park, an airport, a school, or other public facility. The due process, public use, and just compensation requirements of the takings clause (quoted above) mean that government must follow a set of rules—notice, hearings, and witnesses—before taking the property for public use and must pay fair value.

It is easy to see why this power is necessary. Without the power to compel property owners to sell property to them, governments could not accomplish the things we expect them to do. However, what are the limits of this power? What if government actions or rules make property less valuable without formally taking possession of it? Has this property been "taken"? Another question involves what counts as a public use. If the government purchases property and then transfers the property to a private group, which will use or develop the property in a way the government considers beneficial to the community, can it still count as a public use?

We will take these questions one at a time.

First, what is a taking? Some takings are easy to understand—for example, taking land to build a school. When the government physically takes and retains the land, a taking has occurred. In this situation, the government can force landowners to sell but must pay market value for the property.

Zoning, which is regulation limiting the use of buildings or property, is generally not considered a taking. If you live in an area zoned for residential use, you usually cannot operate a business. Zoning regulations can make neighborhoods more pleasant and peaceful or protect sensitive natural environments. But a restrictive zoning regulation can reduce the value of property. Can a zoning regulation be so restrictive that it amounts to a taking? There is no set formula to determining this, but the Supreme Court in a series of cases has determined that a taking need not be physical and that a government action or regulation, which causes a substantial loss of value, use, or enjoyment of your property, can be considered a taking under some circumstances. It could be loss of use of enjoyment of the property through excessive noise caused by military airplanes (*United States v. Causby*, 1946); loss of private, exclusive beachfront access (*Nollan v. California Coastal Commission*, 1987); or loss of value through an environmental regulation that prevents the development of land (*Lucas v. South Carolina Coastal Council*, 1992). On the other hand, a New York City regulation that prevented the owners of Grand Central Terminal from building a skyscraper on top of it was determined not to be a taking (*Penn Central Transportation v. New York City*, 1987).

Whether or not a government regulation amounts to a taking is important, because if it is a taking, the government has to pay for the property, which means the economic cost of the regulation is paid by taxpayers. If it is not a taking, then the cost is borne by the property owner.

Second, what is the public use requirement? The government can only take property for "public use." If the government's purpose is a public use, the government can use its power of eminent domain to force the property owner to sell and will have to pay fair compensation. The definition of public use is broad, but using the property for courthouses, parks, schools, airports, and similar public or quasi-public entities definitely counts. What about urban renewal programs, where the government condemns a badly deteriorated private area and then sells it to a private developer for a governmentally approved project in urban renewal? The

Supreme Court has upheld such takings as falling under a broad definition of public use. For example, in *Berman v. Parker* (1954), the Supreme Court unanimously upheld legislation to redevelop the blighted urban areas of Washington, DC, even though private developers were going to buy the property for redevelopment. The legislature had determined that there was a public purpose to this private redevelopment—to rid Washington, DC, of an urban blight—and the Court deferred to the legislative determination. However, while the Court upheld a similar plan in *Kelo v. City of New London* (2005), the concurring and dissenting opinions suggested that the Court might seek a much more restrictive standard to determine if a taking falls under a "public use." A narrow understanding of "public use" protects property rights, but it also limits the government's ability to use eminent domain for economic purposes.

What is the future of the takings clause? A majority of justices on the current Court are clearly sympathetic to property rights claims. They have expanded what constitutes a taking and appear ready to restrict the meaning of public use. In the short term, at least, we can expect to see more victories for those advocating greater protection of private property.

About the author

Robert Howard is a professor of political science at Georgia State University and the executive director of the Southern Political Science Association. His research interests are courts and public policy and judicial decision-making.

Suggestions for further reading

In this book
See essays 1 (Why Do We Have a Constitution?) and 48 (Homes and the Fourth Amendment).

Elsewhere
Alexander, Gregory, and Eduardo Peñalver. 2012. *An Introduction to Property Theory*. Cambridge: Cambridge University Press. Chap. 8.

Horne v. Department of Agriculture, 576 U.S. 350 (2015).

Kelo v. City of New London, 545 U.S. 469 (2005).

39

Is There a Right to Abortion in the Constitution?

Chase Porter

On May 2, 2022, *Politico* published a leaked first draft of the Supreme Court's majority opinion in *Dobbs v. Jackson Women's Health Organization*. The leak set off multiple firestorms that fundamentally reshaped American politics. Substantively, the draft revealed that the Court was poised to overturn *Roe v. Wade*, erasing the forty-nine-year-old precedent that established the constitutional right to an abortion. A month and a half later, on June 24, five justices did exactly that. By overturning *Roe* and *Planned Parenthood v. Casey*, the Court returned the question of abortion to the individual states. Within hours, various states began to implement "trigger laws" that banned elective abortions if the Court was to ever overturn *Roe*. As it was prior to *Roe*, access to abortions is now a function of where someone is in the United States. Where did *Roe* come from, and where did it go? The answer to that question begins with an arrest.

On November 10, 1961, New Haven police arrested Estelle Griswold and C. Lee Buxton for prescribing birth control, thus violating a Connecticut law that banned contraceptives. Four years later, the Supreme Court overturned the law in *Griswold v. Connecticut* (1965). The majority ruled that the written guarantees in the Bill of Rights should be read broadly to include "penumbras, formed by emanations" that created a right to privacy that protects certain liberties related to personal autonomy. Although the Bill of Rights does not contain the phrase "right to privacy," the guarantees found in various amendments cast a shadow of privacy that covers various behaviors. The usage of contraception is one. In *Roe v. Wade* (1973), the Supreme Court determined that getting an abortion was another.

The Court majority ruled that the extent of the right to an abortion was determined by the timeline of the pregnancy. Under *Roe*, abortions until the end of the first trimester were completely protected as a private medical decision between a woman and her doctor. Any abortions performed after the end of the first trimester were subject to regulations for the protection of maternal health. After "viability," which is the point in pregnancy that the fetus is conceivably able to survive outside of the womb with appropriate medical intervention, there was a compelling state interest in the "potentiality of human life" that allowed states to ban abortions if exceptions were left in the law to preserve the life or health of the mother. In *Planned Parenthood of Southeastern Pennsylvania v. Casey* (1992), the Court simplified the timeline issue. Abortion could be banned postviability with the life/health exception but could only be regulated previability if the regulations did not place an "undue burden" on the right to obtain an abortion.

The right to an abortion was built on the legal concept of substantive due process. According to the Fourteenth Amendment, states cannot infringe on the right to liberty without the due process of law. Starting with *Griswold*, the Court had interpreted that liberty right to include the "substance" of privacy rights (hence the term *substantive*). Over time, the Court expanded the zone of privacy covered by the Fourteenth Amendment to include rights such as abortion and same-sex marriage. However, these rights were unenumerated rights, meaning the rights were not explicitly listed in the text of the Constitution. Justice Alito, writing for the majority in *Dobbs*, argued that because the right to an abortion was unenumerated, it must be justified as a fundamental right by the history and traditions of American law. By the *Dobbs* majority's reading of history, the right was not a fundamental right in American legal history; thus, *Roe* and *Casey* were wrongly decided and must be overturned. Since abortion is not a fundamental right, states are allowed to ban abortions if they can demonstrate a rational basis for so doing. The Court also held that determining when in pregnancy to ban abortion is a matter for states to democratically decide; thus, if a state determines through the legislative process that life begins at conception, for instance, it is now rationally justified in banning abortion from that point forward, since the decision rests with the state. This creates a situation where the right to abortion varies from state to state. Theoretically, the long-standing constitutional right to interstate travel would allow an individual to travel to a state where abortion is legal to obtain one. In a concurrence in *Dobbs*, Justice Kavanaugh explicitly recognized this right. However, interstate travel is an unenumerated right and thus rests on potentially shakier ground than explicitly granted rights. Given Kavanaugh's stated view, the right to interstate travel apparently still enjoys the support of a majority of justices.

Additionally, the Court has previously held that states do not possess the right to punish an individual for a lawful act committed in another state if the act does not affect an individual in the original state. As of this writing, Missouri is the first state to consider legislation that would circumvent this principle by allowing for civil lawsuits against anyone who aids an out-of-state abortion. California implemented a law the day *Dobbs* was released to protect doctors from liability in that instance. In short, there are pragmatic legal questions to be answered.

Justice Alito's logic could open the door to the revocation of other unenumerated rights, but he argued that the logic of the opinion can only be applied to abortion, as abortion is unique in that it involves the taking of a potential life. The dissent observed that Alito's limitation could simply be ignored by future justices and *Dobbs* could be used as a justification to eliminate other rights, such as the right to same-sex marriage. The dissenters also expressed grave concerns about the implications of this decision for the rights and well-being of women. While the majority argued that *Roe* and *Casey* were bad precedents that had to be overturned, the dissent contended that overturning established precedent destabilizes the law. The Court giveth; the Court taketh away; perhaps a future Court will giveth again?

About the author

Chase Porter is an assistant professor of political science at California Baptist University. He specializes in the study of judicial politics and the integration of constitutional law, political theory, religion, and American politics.

Suggestions for further reading

In this book
See essays 1 (Why Do We Have a Constitution?), 6 (How Can We Tell What the Constitution Means?), and 20 (Judicial Review).

Elsewhere
Beckwith, Francis J. 2007. *Defending Life: A Moral and Legal Case against Abortion Choice*. New York: Cambridge University Press.

Hull, N. E. H., and Peter Charles Hoffer. 2021. *Roe v. Wade: The Abortion Rights Controversy in American History*, 3rd ed. Lawrence: University Press of Kansas.

Ziegler, Mary. 2020. *Abortion and the Law in America*. New York: Cambridge University Press.

Equality and Civil Rights

40
How Did the Civil War Amendments Change the Constitution?

Gbemende Johnson

The Declaration of Independence speaks of equality. The preamble of the U.S. Constitution speaks of the "Blessings of Liberty." However, it is the Civil War Amendments that have slowly leaned American democracy toward greater inclusivity and liberty by freeing enslaved individuals (thirteenth), conferring birthright citizenship (fourteenth), and extending the franchise without regard to race or "previous condition of servitude" (fifteenth).

Months prior to the end of the Civil War, Congress passed the Thirteenth Amendment, abolishing slavery, and the amendment was ratified by the states in December 1865, freeing millions of enslaved individuals. The words of the Thirteenth Amendment alone, however, were not sufficient to formally integrate enslaved African Americans into postwar society. Along with the new amendment, the war's end ushered in the Reconstruction era, during which the Republican-majority Congress passed laws such as the Freedmen's Bureau Acts that provided economic, medical, and educational aid to emancipated African Americans. Military enforcement of Reconstruction policies was also central to the implementation of the newly emancipated status of African Americans.

While the abolishment of slavery in its practiced form pushed the Constitution toward the values of equality expressed in the Declaration of Independence, African Americans still lacked citizenship guarantees because of the Supreme Court's earlier ruling in *Dred Scott v. Sanford* (1857). In *Dred Scott*, the Supreme Court stated that African Americans, free or enslaved, were never meant to be citizens. One key aim of the Fourteenth Amendment, ratified in 1868, was to directly overturn this ruling through the establishment of birthright citizenship. The

Fourteenth Amendment also sought to police discriminatory actions by state governments by dictating that a state could not "deprive any person of life, liberty, or property, without due process of law" or deny "equal protection of the laws."

Despite this language, multiple Supreme Court decisions limited the reach of these clauses regarding civil rights for African Americans. For example, in *Plessy v. Ferguson* (1896), the Supreme Court ruled that Louisiana's "separate but equal" segregation policies did not violate the Fourteenth Amendment's equal protection clause. It was only several decades later that the Court began relying on the equal protection clause to actively promote racial equality. Key examples are *Shelley v. Kraemer* (1948), holding that covenants restricting sales of property to African Americans could not legally be enforced, and the line of school desegregation cases that began with *Brown v. Board of Education* (1954).

The Fourteenth Amendment's due process clause created another door through which people could seek protection against the behavior of state and local governments. Today we think of the Bill of Rights as constraining all governments, but it was initially intended to apply only to *federal* government action. In fact, it grew out of a promise made during the ratification debates to placate those suspicious of the Constitution's new powerful central government. (Note that the Bill of Rights begins with the words "Congress shall make no law.") The limited reach of the Bill of Rights was made clear in *Barron v. Baltimore* (1833), where the Supreme Court ruled that the Fifth Amendment was inapplicable to nonfederal government action.

Thirty-five years later, key proponents of the Fourteenth Amendment expected it to make the Bill of Rights applicable to the states. But not everyone shared this view, and the Supreme Court was in no rush to adopt it, as illustrated in the *Slaughter-House Cases* (1873) and the case of *U.S. v. Cruikshank* (1873). In *Cruikshank*, which involved challenges to convictions related to the massacre of African Americans over a disputed election, the Supreme Court ruled that the First and Second Amendments were only applicable to the federal government.

It was nearly sixty years after the passage of the Fourteenth Amendment that the Supreme Court acknowledged that a provision of the Bill of Rights could limit state action in *Gitlow v. New York* (1925). Since then, the voice of the Court has been central in the evolution and impact of the Fourteenth Amendment. Through the process of "selective incorporation," the Court has applied the majority of the Bill of Rights protections to state and local government action. The U.S. Supreme

Court most recently (2010) interpreted the Second Amendment's right to "bear arms" to include protections against state restrictions on gun ownership.

Compared to the broad Fourteenth Amendment, the Fifteenth Amendment, ratified in 1870, had a more focused aim: expanding voting rights. Buttressed with military enforcement, the effects of the Fifteenth Amendment were immediate. Not only did African American men register to vote, but dozens were elected to state legislative bodies, and two African American men, Hiram Revels and Blanche K. Bruce, served in the U.S. Senate. However, similar to the trajectory of the other Civil War Amendments relative to African American advancement, the gains in voting rights met resistance and retrenchment with the end of Reconstruction and the rise of Jim Crow and legalized discrimination. As Democrats retook power in states readmitted to the Union, and with the withdrawal of U.S. troops after the 1876 presidential election, states revised their laws and constitutions to restrict access to the ballot and limit the political, legal, and economic mobility of African Americans. It was not until the passage of the 1965 Voting Rights Act that African Americans could safely and consistently exercise their right to vote.

The Civil War Amendments, while powerful, were not self-enforcing and did not initially provide sustainable legal equality for African Americans. As political conditions and Supreme Court preferences shifted, the reach of the guarantees expressed in the Civil War Amendments have shifted as well. However, advocates for equality and expansive liberties in subsequent generations, who many times fought their battles in court, have appealed to the language and values of the Civil War Amendments as testimony in favor of their cause.

About the author

Gbemende Johnson is an associate professor of political science at the University of Georgia. Her research areas are executive-judicial relations, transparency, and race and politics.

Suggestions for further reading

In this book
See essays 4 (Racism in the Constitution), 37 (Does the Second Amendment Give Me the Right to Carry a Gun?), and 45 (Regulating Private Discrimination).

Elsewhere

Du Bois, W. E. B. 1935. *Black Reconstruction in America 1860–1880*. New York: Free Press.

Foner, Eric. 2019. *The Second Founding: How the Civil War and Reconstruction Remade the Constitution*. New York: W. W. Norton.

Masur, Kate. 2021. *Until Justice Be Done: America's First Civil Rights Movement, from the Revolution to Reconstruction*. New York: W. W. Norton.

41
Who Is a Citizen?

Anna O. Law

Each nation sorts its inhabitants into citizens and noncitizens. Citizenship is not just about having a passport. Nations use the designation of "citizen" to bestow a package of protections, privileges, and immunities. Political theorist Hannah Arendt famously wrote that citizenship means "you have the right to have rights."

The U.S. Constitution, drafted in 1787, is unhelpful in explaining citizenship. There is only one clause found in Article I, Section 8 that states, "[The national Congress shall have exclusive power] to establish a uniform Rule of Naturalization." Naturalization is a legal process by which the government gives a person the same rights and privileges as a native-born citizen.

Under British dominion, all persons in the colonies were subjects of the Crown and Parliament. After the Revolutionary War, Americans created a new political status of a "United States citizen." The move rejected the commonly accepted maxim that allegiance to a sovereign was hereditary and immutable. The Americans emphasized consent. They were forming a sovereign nation whose leaders governed only with the consent of citizens. But also, the nation could draw its boundaries by extending citizenship to some but not others.

At the U.S. founding, enslaved and free Black people were not citizens though most wanted full inclusion and equality. Indians were also not citizens, but most native peoples did not want American citizenship and instead wished for their own independent sovereignty. White women did not have full citizenship rights until the early nineteenth century. It was an uncontroversial belief at the founding among the majority of the U.S. population that full citizenship rights were reserved for white men. Abolitionists, Black people, and later, suffragists vigorously contested that conceptualization. The framers' view was formalized in the Naturalization Act of 1790, which limited naturalization to all "free white person[s]."

The U.S. Constitution created a federal system of government where the national government and states share power. It means that each state can make its own policies regarding citizenship. Federalism allowed the nation to temporarily manage slavery while the nation expanded westward. The arrangement enabled sectional variation and discrimination. Before the Civil War, some northern states allowed Black people to be citizens of the state and to vote. Slave states guaranteed no rights to enslaved Blacks and instead treated them as human property; they also severely limited the rights of free Blacks.

That delicate balancing act was disrupted by a Supreme Court decision, *Dred Scott v. Sanford* (1857), about the legal status of an enslaved man named Dred Scott who was taken by his enslavers to the free state of Illinois and then returned to Missouri, a slave state. Scott claimed he became free when he visited a free state. Chief Justice Roger Taney, writing for the Court majority, disagreed, saying Scott was still enslaved.

Taney went even further, opining that the framers who drafted the U.S. Constitution never consider Blacks, whether enslaved or free, as citizens. Taney's conclusion was that as a noncitizen, Dred Scott did not have the right to petition the Supreme Court for his freedom.

Taney's decision raised the thorny question of the relationship between state and national citizenship. Was Dred Scott, or any person residing in the United States, a citizen only of their home state or also a citizen of the United States? While his citizenship status was clear under Missouri law, did Scott have additional protections as a citizen of the United States?

The incongruities between state and national citizenship were resolved only after a bloody Civil War with the passage of the Thirteenth, Fourteenth, and Fifteenth Amendments, collectively known as the Reconstruction Amendments. Among those, the Fourteenth Amendment specifically grants *jus solis* or "birthright citizenship" to all. That guarantee was to clarify the citizenship status of Blacks. It meant that all persons born on U.S. soil, with narrow exceptions, are automatically U.S. citizens. The equal protection clause of the Fourteenth Amendment further cleared up that national citizenship took precedent over state citizenship.

Despite the magisterial language of the Fourteenth Amendment, the United States did not become a full democracy that honored the rights of all citizens until the passage of the Nineteenth Amendment, giving white women the right to vote in 1920; the 1960s civil rights movement; and the passage of the 1964 Civil Rights Act and 1965 Voting Rights Act.

Because citizenship allows a nation to choose who to grant it to, the United States has selected at various points in immigration history to deny citizenship to certain groups, such as with the 1882 Chinese Exclusion Act that, in addition to barring almost all Chinese migration, reinforced the Naturalization Act of 1790 by explicitly banning Chinese from naturalizing. (The Chinese did not gain naturalization rights until 1943.)

Some immigrants cannot naturalize, but what about their children born on U.S. soil? That question was answered in the Supreme Court case *Wong Kim Ark v. U.S.* (1898). Wong Kim Ark was born in California to two Chinese immigrants who resided in the United States but were barred from naturalizing. Wong was later barred by federal immigration authorities from returning to San Francisco after a trip to China. The Supreme Court ruled that the Fourteenth Amendment's birthright citizenship guarantee extended to children born in the United States to immigrants legally ineligible for naturalization.

American Indians have had a complex legal relationship with U.S. citizenship. Whether Indigenous people had citizenship had been determined at times based on race, relation of individuals to their tribal nations, or marital status. The birthright citizenship clause excluded American Indians from citizenship. Acknowledging the high rates of Indian enlistment in World War I, the Indian Citizenship Act was signed into law by Calvin Coolidge in 1924. That law conferred U.S. citizenship to all Indians born within the geographical U.S. boundaries. This conferral was not uniformly welcomed by American Indian Nations, some of whom viewed the imposition as undercutting native sovereignty.

Citizenship is still contested, and to this day, the United States continues to struggle toward a more perfect union.

About the author

Anna O. Law is the Herbert Kurz Chair in Constitutional Rights and associate professor of political science at CUNY Brooklyn College. Her research and teaching focus on the intersection between law, politics, and U.S. immigration policy history.

Suggestions for further reading

In this book
See essays 22 (Who Can Vote?), 40 (How Did the Civil War Amendments Change the Constitution?), and 42 (Does the Constitution Protect Noncitizens?).

Elsewhere

Kettner, James H. 1978. *The Development of American Citizenship, 1608–1870.* Chapel Hill: University of North Carolina Press.

Nackenoff, Carrol, and Julie Novkov. 2021. *American by Birth: Wong Kim Ark and the Battle for Citizenship.* Lawrence: University Press of Kansas.

Jones, Martha. 2018. *Birthright Citizens: A History of Race and Rights in Antebellum America.* New York: Cambridge University Press.

Witkin, Alexandra. 1995. "To Silence a Drum: The Imposition of United States Citizenship on Native Peoples." *Historical Reflections / Réflexions Historiques* 21, no. 2 (Spring): 353–83.

42
Does the Constitution Protect Noncitizens?

Allen Linken

> All persons born or naturalized in the United States, and subject to the jurisdiction thereof, are citizens of the United States and of the state wherein they reside. No state shall make or enforce any law which shall abridge the privileges or immunities of *citizens* of the United States; nor shall any state deprive *any person* of life, liberty, or property, without due process of law; nor deny to *any person* within its jurisdiction the equal protection of the laws.
>
> —U.S. Constitution, Fourteenth Amendment, Section 1 (emphasis added)

One of the most counterintuitive features of the U.S. Constitution is that it grants rights to noncitizens. That means the Constitution protects the rights of people who don't swear an oath of loyalty to it and even protects people who might attack the United States. This surprising standard is plain in the language of the Fourteenth Amendment quoted above.

After stipulating that all persons born or naturalized in the United States are citizens of the United States, the Fourteenth Amendment lays out three separate rights, found in what are known as the privileges or immunities clause (which rights include the privileges associated with citizenship), the due process clause (which rights include those associated with procedural and substantive fairness), and the equal protection clause (which rights include treating groups as equal under law). It is important to note that each of these clauses applies to different groups of people. The privileges or immunities clause protects only citizens of the United States. The due process clause protects all persons. The equal protection clause applies to any person within a specific jurisdiction (e.g., a state or a city).

There are noncitizens living in every state. The text of the Fourteenth Amendment makes it clear that these noncitizens have a right to due process and to equal protection of the laws. Although the Supreme Court does not always follow the plain language of the Constitution (e.g., the Court has upheld some restrictions on speech despite the First Amendment's prohibition on laws "abridging the freedom of speech"), the Court has generally, through case law, enforced the rights granted to noncitizens with clear, unambiguous language. For example, *Plyler v. Doe* (1982) involved a challenge to a Texas law that allowed local public schools to deny educational services to children of undocumented parents. The Supreme Court declared this law unconstitutional, holding that "whatever his status under the immigration laws, an alien is surely a 'person' in any ordinary sense of that term" (where "person" references the language in the equal protection clause).

While there is a general consensus that for purposes of the due process and equal protection clauses, noncitizens have rights equivalent to those of citizens, there are certain, narrow exceptions to that broad rule. For example, with the equal protection clause at issue in *Ambach v. Norwick* (1979), the Court held that states may prohibit noncitizens from teaching in public schools, as such a position goes "to the heart of a representative government" (though all teachers may not be created equal, as a social studies teacher may be more able to be restricted to citizens than a gym or foreign language teacher, since the social studies teacher is likely more connected to civics and American government than their colleagues).

One of the first cases to examine the coverage of these clauses was *Yick Wo v. Hopkins* (1886). In this case, the Court declared unconstitutional a city ordinance that required all laundries in wooden buildings to hold permits. Although this law did not explicitly discriminate against noncitizens, the Court found that no laundries owned by people of Chinese descent were granted permits, despite them owning nearly 90 percent of the laundries in the city. In the opinion to that case, the Court wrote that "the Fourteenth Amendment . . . is not confined to the protection of citizens" and that as it regards the equal protection of the laws, the rights of one person in a jurisdiction are required to be the same as the rights of another, regardless of citizenship. Here, the language in the opinion exactly mirrors the text of the Constitution; while noncitizens can be barred from the privileges and immunities of the United States, they can't be barred from equal protection of the law within a specific jurisdiction. Because the ordinance, in practice, wasn't treating all owners as equal under the law, the law was ruled to be unconstitutional.

A more recent and dramatic example of noncitizens being protected by the Constitution (in this case, by filing a writ of habeas corpus instead of through the Fourteenth Amendment) is that of Salim Hamdan, who was the bodyguard and chauffeur to Osama bin Laden. Hamdan was captured and sent to a U.S. detention facility at Guantanamo Bay, Cuba. A commission set up to review detainees determined that Hamdan was an "enemy combatant." Hamdan challenged that determination. In response to that challenge, the Supreme Court, in *Hamdan v. Rumsfeld* (2006), ruled that because the military commissions were not properly authorized under U.S. law, they could not be used to try Hamdan. The point of this example is that even a noncitizen working for a terrorist organization that had attacked the United States has rights under the Constitution and laws of the United States. The text of the Constitution is clear on this point.

About the author

Allen Linken is an associate professor of political science at the University of Alabama. He works primarily on judicial decision-making and civil-military relations.

Suggestions for further reading

In this book
See essays 22 (Who Can Vote?), 40 (How Did the Civil War Amendments Change the Constitution?), and 41 (Who Is a Citizen?).

Elsewhere
Yick Wo v. Hopkins, 118 U.S. 356 (1886): Distinctions among individuals for different clauses in the Fourteenth Amendment.

Ex parte Quirin, 317 U.S. 1 (1942): Enemy combatants (who may or not be American citizens) have the right to challenge the constitutionality of their charges.

Reno v. Flores, 507 U.S. 292 (1993): Constitutional provisions, other than the Fourteenth Amendment, apply to noncitizens. In this case, the Fifth Amendment entitled aliens to due process of law in deportation proceedings.

43

Does the Equal Protection Clause Cover Gender?

Laura P. Moyer

What does the U.S. Constitution have to say about gender discrimination? Well, if you search the Constitution, you will find only one reference to gender in the entire document, and that is in the Nineteenth Amendment. Ratified in 1920, this amendment states that "the right of citizens of the United States to vote shall not be denied or abridged by the United States or by any state on account of sex" and gives Congress the power to enforce this provision through passing laws. That's it—no other mentions of women or gender discrimination at all. And the Nineteenth Amendment really did not give all women the right to vote, since African American women still faced discrimination at the ballot box because of Jim Crow laws.

So does this mean that the Constitution placed no limits on gender discrimination? Practically, the answer to this question was "yes" all the way up to the 1970s.

Here's why. The United States inherited legal traditions from English law that limited women's rights, and these were influential in shaping all kinds of state and federal laws. One important concept from English law was called *coverture*, a doctrine that meant women lost their separate legal existence after they were married. This affected women's ability to own property, to be financially independent, to enter into contracts, to receive protection from domestic violence, to participate in politics, and to hold certain occupations, among other things.

In 1873, Myra Bradwell challenged one such state law that prevented women from becoming lawyers—but in *Bradwell v. Illinois* (1873), the Supreme Court ruled that the Fourteenth Amendment did not protect women facing this discrimination. One justice even wrote that women's destiny was to fulfill "the noble and benign offices of wife and mother."

A century later, the ACLU Women's Rights Project and attorney (and future Supreme Court justice) Ruth Bader Ginsburg took an incremental approach to challenging gender discrimination before the Supreme Court. In a series of cases, they successfully argued that when laws are based on gender stereotypes rather than individual abilities, this violates the constitutional guarantee of equal protection of the law in the Fifth and Fourteenth Amendments—the same parts of the Constitution that had been used to dismantle racial segregation.

A key part of this legal strategy was to take cases in which men also faced discrimination—an insightful move, given the all-male composition of the Supreme Court at the time. For instance, in *Weinberger v. Wiesenfeld* (1974), the Court struck down a provision of the Social Security Act that provided benefits to widowed mothers, but not widowed fathers, caring for children.

One complicating factor for the Supreme Court during the early 1970s was the Equal Rights Amendment (ERA). This proposed constitutional amendment was passed out of Congress with overwhelming support and moved to the states for ratification in 1972. Some members of the Supreme Court were of the opinion that it was unnecessary for the Court to interpret the Constitution to protect against gender discrimination, given that the ERA was imminent and would essentially do the work for them. But there was one problem: the ERA fell three votes short of ratification in the states.

So it was left up to the Supreme Court. In *Craig v. Boren* (1976), the court adopted a new test, called intermediate scrutiny, that makes it harder for government actors to justify laws that treat individuals differently on account of their sex. Under this new legal standard, the Constitution's Fifth and Fourteenth Amendments have become important tools in addressing gender discrimination in state and federal laws, though these provisions do not apply to discrimination by nongovernmental actors like private employers.

How does intermediate scrutiny work in practice? Under this test, the Supreme Court has struck down state policies that admit only women or only men to public universities when those policies are based on stereotypes about the abilities of men and women. On the other hand, the Supreme Court upheld the all-male military draft under intermediate scrutiny and recently declined to hear a new challenge to overturn this precedent. In *Rostker v. Goldberg* (1981), the Court concluded that Congress had made a reasoned judgment about draft eligibility based on women's (then) exclusion from combat positions—rather than basing the policy on outmoded gender stereotypes.

There are a few other limitations to how the equal protection clause has been interpreted with respect to gender. One area is transgender rights, although some protections do exist under federal statutes and laws in some states. Another area is abortion. When the Supreme Court recognized in *Roe v. Wade* (1973) that women have a constitutional right to an abortion, they based that right on a right to privacy from another part of the Constitution rather than linking it to the equal protection clause.

Beyond the Constitution, other laws at the international, federal, and state levels protect against gender discrimination. For instance, Congress passed Title IX to address gender discrimination in education, and about half of all states have provisions in their state constitutions or state laws addressing discrimination based on sex.

In sum, although the constitutional text says almost nothing about gender, broad judicial interpretations have extended the concept of equal protection to both men and women.

About the author

Laura P. Moyer is an associate professor of political science at the University of Louisville. Her research focuses on gender, race, and the judiciary.

Suggestions for further reading

In this book
See essays 22 (Who Can Vote?) and 40 (How Did the Civil War Amendments Change the Constitution?).

Elsewhere
https://www.aclu.org/other/about-aclu-womens-rights-project—A history of the ACLU Women's Rights Project.

https://draftingtable.constitutioncenter.org/item/19th-amendment—The Constitution Center's resources on the Nineteenth Amendment.

Ginsburg, Ruth Bader, and Amanda L. Tyler. 2021. *Justice, Justice Thou Shalt Pursue: A Life's Work Fighting for a More Perfect Union.* Oakland: University of California Press.

44
Equal Protection beyond Race and Sex

David E. Klein

The equal protection clause of the Fourteenth Amendment, ratified in the aftermath of the Civil War, was clearly intended to combat racial discrimination. However, its terms are general: "No state shall . . . deny to any person within its jurisdiction the equal protection of the laws." In fact, there is no mention of either race or skin color in the entire amendment. People who feel they face governmental discrimination on other grounds have long argued that the clause should protect them too.

Laura P. Moyer's essay describes how the clause came to be applied to gender discrimination. This essay considers other possible applications. May a state require judges to step down when they turn seventy? Is it permissible to restrict transgender students' participation in high school sports? Do driving fees and fine structures unconstitutionally discriminate against people with limited incomes?

There is no room to tackle these questions individually in such a brief essay, but it is possible to identify a general framework in which to analyze them. Because we tend to see the term "discrimination" as pejorative, we should start by reminding ourselves that there are many occasions when it is perfectly appropriate for a government to distinguish between people. For instance, when hiring teachers, a government may properly favor applicants who have never committed violent crimes. It may properly limit assistance programs to people who are most in need.

Judges have struggled through the years to define precise tests for when governmental discrimination is permissible. But in the end, the question almost always comes down to whether the danger of a certain way of categorizing people outweighs whatever good the government aims to accomplish.

When it comes to invidious discrimination, race is the paradigmatic case. The rationales that were once offered for distinguishing between races are now almost universally regarded as bogus. And they were used to justify the worst things Americans have ever done to one another, from enslavement to murder. Because of this terrible history, the Supreme Court eventually came to conclude that the government should almost never be permitted to treat people differently because of race. It therefore erected a very high bar. Laws or government actions that treat some people better than others because of their race are only permissible if they serve a "compelling" interest and that interest couldn't be promoted as effectively through a policy that ignored race. (Today, only some carefully delineated affirmative action programs are permitted.)

If you oppose some other way of differentiating between people, you want to see courts apply this same "strict scrutiny" to the objectionable policies. For this to happen, you would need to persuade them that this other form of categorization is as insidious as race, or at least nearly so. So far, the Supreme Court has only been persuaded to extend strict scrutiny to the closely related categories of national origin and citizenship. (It also applies strict scrutiny to laws targeted at specific religions, though here the free exercise clause also plays a role.)

Advocates have come close with two other categories—sex/gender and legitimacy. The Court considers these categories to have slightly greater validity than race (for instance, in the area of parental rights) but recognizes that they have often been abused. It therefore subjects policies that rely on these categories to a test, sometimes called "intermediate scrutiny," that is not as onerous as strict scrutiny but does present a significant hurdle for the government to overcome.

That the Court has not singled out other ways of differentiating between people for special scrutiny does not mean that governments are free to rely on those other classifications whenever and however they like. For one thing, they could join the Court's "suspect" list in the future.

This seems especially likely for sexual orientation. A majority of the Court has shown considerable sympathy for claims of discrimination in the past two decades. Furthermore, in *Bostock v. Clayton County* (2020), the Court ruled that the Civil Rights Act of 1964's prohibition of employment discrimination on the basis of sex necessarily prohibits discrimination on the basis of sexual orientation as well. Although this case involved the interpretation of a statute, rather than the Constitution, its logic could easily transfer. Its logic could also be extended to protect transgender people.

Even when relying on a category that the Court has not recognized as especially dubious, the government must be able to show that a challenged policy or practice is rationally related to a legitimate state interest. This rules out discrimination based solely on hostility toward a particular group. For example, while states might successfully defend policies limiting the participation of transgender athletes, laws prohibiting transgender people from being teachers or owning businesses would have no chance of being upheld in court. The Constitution does not bar states from setting mandatory retirement ages for some government positions, but it does bar them from forcing people over a certain age to exit the workforce entirely. States may not have to take income into account when setting fine levels for traffic violations, but they cannot mandate a minimum income for driving a car.

In each example where a policy would be disallowed under the equal protection clause, it is evident that the intense harm caused to the targeted group, together with the moral cost to society of violating the principle of equality, would outweigh whatever benefits the restrictions might bring. It is difficult to predict what specific policies will and won't be permitted in the future: these will keep changing as we reassess the validity and utility of different ways of categorizing people. But we can be confident that the clause's scope will continue to extend far beyond the specific evil it was designed to combat.

About the author

David E. Klein is a professor of political science at Eastern Michigan University. His work focuses primarily on judicial decision-making and the development of the law.

Suggestions for further reading

In this book
See essays 40 (How Did the Civil War Amendments Change the Constitution?), 43 (Does the Equal Protection Clause Cover Gender?), and 47 (Is There a Right to Same-Sex Marriage?).

Elsewhere
Fallon, Richard H., Jr. 2007. "Strict Judicial Scrutiny." *UCLA Law Review* 54:1267–1337.

Clark v. Jeter, 486 U.S. 456 (1988).

Graham v. Richardson, 403 U.S. 365 (1971).

45

Regulating Private Discrimination

Karen Swenson

> No state shall . . . deny to any person within its jurisdiction the equal protection of the laws.
>
> —U.S. Constitution, Fourteenth Amendment

> The Congress shall have power . . . to regulate commerce with foreign nations, and among the several states, and with the Indian tribes.
>
> —U.S. Constitution, Article I, Section 8, Clause 3

The Constitution's most important protections from discrimination place limits on governments, not private parties. The Bill of Rights starts with the words "Congress shall make no law." Its reference to the "state" in the Fourteenth Amendment is unambiguous. The only important exception is the Thirteenth Amendment, which abolishes slavery: it is not specific and thus applies to all. Beyond engaging in this abomination, a private actor is free to discriminate and not run afoul of the Constitution!

Demonstrating this, the Supreme Court ruled in *Moose Lodge No. 107 v. Irvis* (1972) that the Moose Lodge could enforce its "whites only" policy and refuse to serve Leroy Irvis, the African American guest of a white lodge member. The lodge held a state-issued liquor license, but this was not sufficient to bring it within the Constitution's restrictions. The Court was concerned about maintaining a meaningful distinction between what is private conduct and what is government action, calling this an "essential dichotomy" with a legacy dating back to the era when the Fourteenth Amendment was ratified.

There are loopholes in the state action doctrine that allow private parties to be sued for violating the Constitution. For instance, private actors in a relationship with the state may be found to be state actors if the two entities bestow on each other significant mutual benefits. This was true of the Eagle Coffee Shoppe, which was located within a city-owned and -maintained parking garage and paid rent to the city, according to *Burton v. Wilmington Parking Authority* (1961). But the general rule is that the Constitution only constrains the behavior of governments and government officials.

Thus, it is incumbent on federal, state, and local legislatures to protect people from private discrimination if that is to happen. Congress did this in 1964 with the landmark Civil Rights Act. Private employers, and private businesses that accommodate the public (such as restaurants, hotels, buses, and swimming pools), cannot discriminate on the basis of race. The act also bans employment discrimination because of an individual's race, color, national origin, religion, or gender. In *Bostock v. Clayton County* (2020), the Court interpreted gender discrimination to include employment discrimination on the basis of sexual orientation and transgender status. Important federal legislation also protects people from private (as well as public) discrimination on the basis of age and disability.

Congress's power to combat private discrimination has not been free of constitutional controversy. A bulwark principle of limited government is that Congress's power to pass legislation is restricted to the specific provisions in Article I, Section 8 *and* the legislation-enabling provisions of the amendments. One such enabling provision is Section 5 of the Fourteenth Amendment, which provides Congress "the power to enforce, by appropriate legislation, the provisions of" the amendment. But if the Fourteenth Amendment does not reach private discrimination under the state action doctrine, can Congress use its enforcement power to legislate against private discrimination? No, the Court held in 1883, and this principle still holds.

So where does Congress's power to combat discrimination come from? From its authority to regulate interstate commerce, as the Court ruled in *Heart of Atlanta Motel, Inc. v. U.S.* (1964). The commerce clause was included in Article I, Section 8 of the Constitution to correct one of the many flaws of the Articles of Confederation: states' destructive squabbling among themselves with trade barriers and restrictions. By the twentieth century, the Court recognized its application to activities that are not primarily about the buying and selling of goods and services. The commerce clause allows Congress to regulate almost whatever it wants, as long as there is some interstate component to the activity. Though the framers may be rolling in their graves at what now qualifies as "interstate commerce," others see the expansion of Congress's powers as necessary. Congress is thus free to eradicate the moral and social evil of private racial discrimination under the guise of regulating commerce. The same expansive reading of the commerce clause allows Congress to ban lottery tickets and harmful drugs, such as marijuana and at least forty additional "controlled substances."

State and local governments are not similarly limited by the federal constitution; the Court recognizes that they have broad "police powers" to protect public health, safety, and welfare. State and local legislation is the bulkhead protecting LGBT people from much discrimination by private businesses. Civil rights remedies are available to people in the LGBT community in some 22 states and 330 municipalities. This still leaves a significant portion of the population unprotected from discrimination by places of public accommodation, however.

Beyond questions of governmental authority, regulations of private discrimination also raise questions about the rights of those whose behavior is regulated. What about the private business owner who wishes not to do business with same-sex couples on the grounds of offense to their First Amendment ideals (whether rooted in religion or creative expression)? Are they entitled to an exemption from the civil rights law? Here we have a clash of cherished values that has yet to be definitively resolved by the Court. Jack Phillips, the owner of Masterpiece Cakeshop, refused to create a wedding cake for Charlie Craig and David Mullins. Phillips was punished by the state of Colorado, and this penalty was reversed by the Court in *Masterpiece Cakeshop v. Colorado Civil Rights Commission* (2018) on the narrow grounds of the hostile treatment Phillips received by the sanctioning body.

The Court also ruled in *Fulton v. City of Philadelphia* (2021) that church-operated adoption agencies under government contract may refuse to work with same-sex couples; in this instance, adoption agencies were not considered to be places of public accommodation and thus not governed by the city of Philadelphia's antidiscrimination ordinance. These cases demonstrate that, at least when it comes to the free exercise clause, the Court is sympathetic to claims that government regulation of private discrimination can go too far.

About the author

Karen Swenson is a professor in the political science department at Eastern Illinois University and serves as the university's prelaw advisor. She studies American courts at all levels.

Suggestions for further reading

In this book
See essays 9 (What Is "Commerce among the Several States," and Why Does It Matter?) and 36 (Does a Twitter Ban Violate the Constitution?).

Elsewhere
https://www.lgbtmap.org/equality-maps—Movement Advancement Project information on state and local LGBTQ equality laws.

Shah, Sohil. 2014. "Free Speech, Football, and Freedom: Why the NFL Should Not Compel Its Players to Speak to the Media." *Texas Review of Entertainment & Sports Law* 16:43–50.

NeJaime, Douglas, and Reva Siegel. 2018. "Religious Exemptions and Antidiscrimination Law in Masterpiece Cakeshop." *Yale Law Journal* 128:201–24.

46

Does the Constitution Permit Affirmative Action?

Kyla K. Stepp

The constitutionality of affirmative action is a relatively recent question, as the U.S. Supreme Court did not begin to examine it until the 1970s. Since that time, the Court has weighed in on this issue many times, its decisions evolving with changes in society and changes in the makeup of the Court. This has not been an easy issue for the Court over the years, as the Court's decisions have almost always been split, often with strong rhetoric on both sides by the justices. The intense division and rhetoric from the Court mirror the public debate over affirmative action.

Although the Court's rulings on affirmative action can be complex and confusing, the general debate over affirmative action is fairly straightforward. Proponents of affirmative action assert that it is desirable for two important reasons. First, centuries of pervasive discrimination against minorities, from slavery to Jim Crow laws to systemic discrimination in employment and higher education, have resulted in unequal opportunities for minorities. Second, proponents argue that diversity is vital in certain environments, particularly on college campuses and in classrooms. These two reasons go hand in hand because affirmative action programs may be the only way to ensure diversity in those environments with a history of discrimination and unequal opportunities for minorities.

Opponents of affirmative action policies assert that such policies discriminate unfairly against nonminority candidates; this is often called "reverse discrimination." They argue that race should never be a consideration in employment, contracting, education, or anything else, and that processes for hiring, contracting, and admissions should be entirely color-blind. They argue that affirmative action policies violate the equal protection clause of the Fourteenth Amendment because they prioritize people according to race.

As with all political hot-button issues, the Supreme Court's job is not to weigh in on the morality of affirmative action policies but only to decide whether such policies are constitutional. The Court first addressed the constitutionality of affirmative action in the 1978 case *Regents of the University of California v. Bakke*. Allan Bakke was a white male who was denied admission to the medical school at the University of California-Davis. He sued the school, claiming that less-qualified minority students were accepted in front of him under the school's affirmative action program, which reserved sixteen seats out of one hundred in its entering classes for minority students.

Bakke won his case, but the Court's ruling was complex and divided. The court held that affirmative action programs are subject to the same "strict scrutiny" as any other policy distinguishing between people on the basis of race: the policy must be in pursuit of a "compelling interest" and must achieve that interest through "narrowly tailored" means. The Court held that public universities do have a compelling interest in achieving a diverse student body. However, the university could not show that its policy of reserving a certain number of seats for minority students was narrowly tailored to achieve a diverse student body; thus, the use of racial quotas was deemed impermissible by the Court.

In the aftermath of the *Bakke* decision, many lawsuits were filed challenging affirmative action programs in public education, as well as in government employment and contracting. The Court initially took a more sympathetic approach to government employment and contracting programs than they had to higher education programs, allowing "quotas" in the form of minority set-aside programs, especially when such programs were adopted to counteract the effects of years of discriminatory practices by a city or state governmental agency. However, in the late 1980s and early 1990s, the Court began to shift away from its acceptance of such programs, even striking down programs very similar in nature to the types they upheld in earlier cases. By 1995, when the Court invalidated a federal contract bonus for minority-owned businesses in *Adarand Constructors, Inc. v. Pena*, it was clear that opponents of affirmative action had successfully convinced a majority of the Court that such programs were no longer necessary to combat discrimination in government employment and contracting.

Interestingly, while the Court has effectively reversed course on the constitutionality of government employment and contracting programs, it has been remarkably consistent in its approach to higher education affirmative action programs since *Bakke*. Many legal scholars and commentators predicted that when the Court turned its attention back to higher education, affirmative action programs would find disfavor with the Court just as employment and contracting programs had. Instead, the Court has repeatedly held that public universities have a compelling interest in maintaining a diverse student body and can use minority status as a factor in admissions, as long as they do not use racial quotas or award "admissions points" for minority status. Most recently, in *Fisher v. University of Texas* (2016), the Court once again (narrowly) upheld the use of affirmative action programs by public universities to ensure diversity in its student population but only if race and other diversity factors are part of a holistic review of applicants for admission.

The debate over affirmative action continues today, primarily in the arena of higher education, as the majority of public universities utilize affirmative action programs for admission to college and to graduate school, including law school and medical school. The Court's decision in *Fisher* was handed down just seven years ago, and although the precedent set by *Fisher* still stands, the makeup of the Court has substantially changed since 2016. Four new justices now sit on the Court, three of whom are considered ideologically conservative. Thus, it is possible that the next time the Court hears an affirmative action case, it may change its answer to the question "Does the Constitution allow affirmative action?" For now, the answer is still a conditional "yes," as long as the policy meets the specific requirements laid out by the Court.

About the author

Kyla K. Stepp is an assistant professor of political science at Central Michigan University. Her research focuses on the intersection of constitutional law, including civil liberties and civil rights, with politics and public policy.

Suggestions for further reading

In this book
See essays 4 (Racism in the Constitution) and 40 (How Did the Civil War Amendments Change the Constitution?).

Elsewhere
Curry, George E., ed. 1996. *The Affirmative Action Debate*. Reading, MA: Addison-Wesley.

Fisher v. University of Texas, 136 S. Ct. 2198 (2016).

47
Is There a Right to Same-Sex Marriage?

Robert J. Hume

Is there a constitutional right to same-sex marriage? When the Supreme Court ruled in *Obergefell v. Hodges* (2015) that states cannot refuse marriage licenses to gay couples, some people found the decision surprising because nowhere does the text of the Constitution or its amendments clearly provide for it. In fact, you will not find mention of any right to marry at all.

Unlike other guarantees, such as freedom of speech and protections against unreasonable searches and seizures, the right to marry the partner of one's choice is an unenumerated right. It is unstated but based on a plausible interpretation of the constitutional text. Like other rights, unenumerated rights have the full force of law.

The Fourteenth Amendment requires that "no state . . . deprive any person of life, liberty, or property, without due process of law." Like much of the Constitution, the language of the Fourteenth Amendment is vague: we know it protects "liberty" but not what liberty is and when a state can impose on it.

The question in *Obergefell* was whether the right to same-sex marriage is among the liberty protections of the Fourteenth Amendment. Specifically, the justices considered whether the right to same-sex marriage is a fundamental right. Most of the time, when states restrict our liberty, due process requires that states have a rational basis for doing so. But when states infringe on fundamental rights, due process requires something more: legislation must be narrowly tailored to achieving a compelling state interest. In other words, states cannot restrict our fundamental rights unless they have very good reasons.

The Supreme Court developed a formula for identifying fundamental rights in *Palko v. Connecticut* (1937), defining fundamental liberty interests as those that are "implicit in the concept of ordered liberty." Such rights are "so rooted in the traditions and conscience of our people as to be ranked as fundamental." In practice, justices look to history and tradition to determine which liberties our society deems fundamental. In doing so, some justices emphasize the Constitution's origins and the country's early history. Others focus more on contemporary or emerging perspectives, on the view that traditions evolve and that society's understanding of the meaning of liberty can change.

Prior to *Obergefell*, the Court had ruled that the due process clause prevented states from criminalizing consensual gay sexual activity. In *Lawrence v. Texas* (2003), the Supreme Court decided that such legislation was demeaning to the "autonomy of self" and the "liberty of the person both in its spatial and more transcendent dimensions." Writing for the majority, Justice Anthony Kennedy acknowledged that American society had long stigmatized gay people but that in recent decades, laws and traditions were changing.

By the time the issue of marriage equality reached the Supreme Court, societal attitudes about same-sex marriage had changed as well. A number of states had legalized same-sex marriage, beginning with Massachusetts in 2004, and after 2011, national majorities were also in favor of legalizing same-sex marriage. Two years before *Obergefell*, in *U.S. v. Windsor* (2013), the Supreme Court struck down the Defense of Marriage Act, which had defined marriage as the union of one man and one woman for purposes of federal law.

Once again writing for the majority in *Obergefell*, Justice Kennedy decided that society now understood that denying gay couples the right to marry was inconsistent with the meaning of liberty protected by the Fourteenth Amendment. "The limitation of marriage to opposite-sex couples may long have seemed natural and just," he wrote, "but its inconsistency with the central meaning of the fundamental right to marry is now manifest." Justice Kennedy reasoned that denying gay couples access to marriage deprived them of basic rights to autonomy and personal choice that were intrinsic to the meaning of liberty. It stigmatized the intimate personal associations of gay people. And it excluded gay partners and their children from the stability, recognition, and benefits that flowed from the institution of marriage.

Not all the justices agreed with the majority in *Obergefell*. In dissent, Chief Justice John Roberts thought the Court had overstepped its authority by deciding that the meaning of the Fourteenth Amendment had changed. "The majority's decision is an act of will, not legal judgment," he wrote. "The right it announces has no basis in the Constitution or this Court's precedent." Writing separately, Justice Scalia accused the majority of "hubris" for choosing to define liberty itself instead of letting the American people decide. In response, Justice Kennedy denied that the Court's decision was premature or lacked a democratic foundation. "There have been referenda, legislative debates, and grassroots campaigns, as well as countless studies, papers, books, and other popular and scholarly writings," he wrote.

The Court had less to say about how to balance same-sex marriage rights against other rights, such as the free exercise of religion. Justice Kennedy acknowledged, "The First Amendment ensures that religious organizations and persons are given proper protection as they seek to teach the principles that are so fulfilling and so central to their lives and faiths." The Court left it for future cases to resolve these and other conflicts between civil rights laws and religious organizations that have conscientious objections to gay unions.

Such litigation has already come to the Supreme Court. *Masterpiece Cakeshop v. Colorado Civil Rights Commission* (2018) concerned a baker who refused to design wedding cakes for same-sex couples because of religious objections. *Fulton v. City of Philadelphia* (2021) focused on Catholic Social Services' refusal to certify same-sex couples as foster parents. In both cases, the Supreme Court avoided the central issue by resolving the cases on narrower grounds.

When the justices do address the core conflict between gay rights and religious freedom, they must decide what the Fourteenth Amendment's guarantee of "liberty" requires and what process is due when states abrogate one liberty in favor of another. Without clear answers in the Constitution, the Court must look beyond the text to identify and define fundamental rights, both enumerated and unenumerated.

About the author

Robert J. Hume is a professor of political science at Fordham University. He focuses on law and policy.

Suggestions for further reading

In this book

See essays 6 (How Can We Tell What the Constitution Means?), 7 (Is the Constitution What the Justices Say It Is?), and 39 (Is There a Right to Abortion in the Constitution?).

Elsewhere

Lawrence v. Texas, 539 U.S. 558 (2003).

Obergefell v. Hodges, 576 U.S. 644 (2015).

The Criminal
Justice Process

48
Homes and the Fourth Amendment

Pamela C. Corley

> The right of the people to be secure in their persons, houses, papers, and effects, against unreasonable searches and seizures, shall not be violated, and no Warrants shall issue, but upon probable cause, supported by Oath or affirmation, and particularly describing the place to be searched, and the persons or things to be seized.
>
> —U.S. Constitution, Fourth Amendment

You may have heard the phrase "A man's house is his castle." In fact, the words of the Fourth Amendment specifically protect "houses, papers, and effects." And the U.S. Supreme Court has recognized that the Fourth Amendment gives the home special protection. For example, in *Florida v. Jardines* (2013), the Court acknowledged that a person has "the right . . . to retreat into his own home and there be free from unreasonable governmental intrusion." But what does that mean? When can the police just come into your home and search if you don't want them to? The Supreme Court, when deciding what the Fourth Amendment means, balances the need of the police to detect and investigate crime against the privacy you have in your home.

Obviously, the police can come into your home and search when they have a valid search warrant. But what about when they don't have a warrant?

Let's say the police are chasing a suspected robber who ran into his house a few minutes earlier. While they're looking for him, they find and seize evidence connected to the robbery along with two guns. The police didn't have a search warrant, but the Supreme Court held, in *Warden v. Hayden* (1967), that they didn't need a warrant, since they were in "hot pursuit." However, the Court found that there was a limit to this hot pursuit exception in *Lange v. California* (2021). In *Lange*, the Court stated that if the person fleeing was suspected of committing a misdemeanor instead of a felony, the hot pursuit exception didn't automatically apply, in part because the home deserves special protection under the Fourth Amendment. Specifically, "officers must respect the sanctity of the home."

What about if the police have probable cause to believe that a person is dealing drugs from his apartment and that the suspected drug dealer knows the police are following him? Are the police allowed to enter the home without a warrant, since they believe he will get rid of the drugs? According to *Ker v. California* (1963), the answer is yes. Since failing to act will lead to evidence being destroyed, the police are allowed to enter the apartment without a warrant.

Another situation that allows the police to enter a house without a warrant is when they need to give emergency aid. In *Brigham City v. Stuart* (2006), police officers were responding to a call about a loud party. They saw through the windows and screen door some adults trying to restrain a juvenile, but then the juvenile broke free and hit one of the adults in the face, and the officers saw blood. One officer went into the house, and the Court held that no warrant was needed to enter.

All of these situations were considered "exigent circumstances." Basically, if there's an emergency, that means that the police must act immediately, and so it wouldn't make sense for them to take the time to get a warrant before entering the house. Since the Fourth Amendment only protects people from "unreasonable" searches and seizures, there are times when an emergency means the police are acting reasonably, even when they don't have a search warrant.

However, even though the police may be allowed to enter your home, where and what they can search for is limited. For example, if the police enter your home under the hot pursuit exception, the police may not search anywhere they want to but only areas where the suspect or weapons may be hidden. In other words, where the police can search is limited by the emergency that justifies the entry in the first place.

And if there is not an emergency situation, the police are not allowed to enter your home without a valid search warrant. In those cases, the Court has found that the needs of police do not justify that invasion of privacy in the home. In fact, the front porch is considered part of the home, and it also receives protection under the Fourth Amendment. In *Jardines*, the police brought a trained drug-detection dog onto the front porch of a house, and the dog indicated that there were drugs inside the house. Even though ordinary citizens are typically invited to come onto the front porch, like Girl Scouts or neighbors, the Supreme Court decided that the police went there to search, which is not part of the typical invitation, and so they needed a search warrant.

About the author

Pamela C. Corley is an associate professor of political science at Southern Methodist University. She specializes in judicial politics.

Suggestions for further reading

In this book
See essays 49 (Automobiles and the Fourth Amendment), 50 (Electronic Surveillance and Tracking), and 53 (Why Do Courts Throw Out Good Evidence?).

Elsewhere
Brigham City v. Stuart, 547 U.S. 398 (2006).

Florida v. Jardines, 569 U.S. 1 (2013).

Lange v. California, 141 S. Ct. 2011 (2021).

49

Automobiles and the Fourth Amendment

Melinda Gann Hall

The right of the people to be secure in their persons, houses, papers, and effects, against unreasonable searches and seizures, shall not be violated, and no Warrants shall issue, but upon probable cause, supported by Oath or affirmation, and particularly describing the place to be searched, and the persons or things to be seized.

—U.S. Constitution, Fourth Amendment

While driving, do you occasionally exceed the speed limit, fail to stop completely at stop signs, accelerate at yellow lights, or check your cell phone while driving? Ever have a fender bender or other crash? And for the less law abiding, do you drive while impaired or transport illegal drugs, stolen property, or other contraband in your vehicle?

If you answered in the affirmative to any of these questions, you are likely to attract the attention of law enforcement at some point in your life and may become the subject of a search. At that time, you will likely ask yourself what the police have the right to examine. Your briefcase, purse, or backpack? Luggage, boxes, or other containers in the vehicle? The trunk, center console, or under the seats? The answers turn on the language of the Fourth Amendment and the Supreme Court's decisions applying the Fourth Amendment to automobiles.

Although automobiles did not exist at the time the Fourth Amendment was adopted, the Fourth Amendment protects "persons, houses, papers, and effects" from "unreasonable searches and seizures" by law enforcement. "Effects" include various modes of transportation, including automobiles. What makes a search reasonable or unreasonable? This can often be ambiguous, which is why so many court cases have been decided on this issue.

Generally, searches are reasonable when conducted pursuant to a warrant based on probable cause. Even so, the absence of a warrant does not make a search inherently unreasonable. In fact, most searches and seizures are made without warrants. The Supreme Court has recognized that some circumstances necessitate exceptions to the warrant requirement in order to protect society and law enforcement. Automobiles are one such exception because, among other things, they can easily be moved. As the Supreme Court explained about automobiles in *Carroll v. United States* (1925), "It is not practicable to secure a warrant because the vehicle can be quickly moved out of the locality or jurisdiction in which the warrant must be sought" (p. 153).

In *Carroll*, the Supreme Court defined the automobile exception in a seemingly straightforward way: the warrantless searches of automobiles, including places in vehicles not in plain sight, are reasonable based on probable cause. In *Carroll*, the Court allowed the warrantless search of a car on a public highway when federal agents had probable cause to believe that the vehicle was transporting illegal liquor during Prohibition. In this search, the contraband alcohol was found only after agents ripped out the upholstery.

Although in *Carroll* the Supreme Court interpreted the Fourth Amendment to allow for the warrantless searches of automobiles, the Court also emphasized that the standard for obtaining a warrant— probable cause—still must be present. With automobiles, probable cause exists when the facts and circumstances lead a reasonable person to believe that the vehicle contains contraband or evidence of a crime. As a legal standard, probable cause is more than a hunch or suspicion but is less than guilt beyond a reasonable doubt, which is required for conviction.

Later in *Chambers v. Maroney* (1970), the Supreme Court upheld the warrantless search of a vehicle no longer at risk of being moved. In this case, police stopped several people in a vehicle and arrested them. The car was then taken to the police station and searched there. The automobile had been used earlier that day by the arrestees in the robbery of a gas station, and police found weapons and stolen property concealed under the dashboard. The Court reasoned that the vehicle could have been searched at the time of the arrest based on probable cause and thus a search later at the station met Fourth Amendment standards.

Through subsequent decisions, the Supreme Court clarified a second justification, implicit in *Chambers*, for the automobile exception: a reduced expectation of privacy. As explained in *Cardwell v. Lewis* (1974),

One has a lesser expectation of privacy in a motor vehicle because its function is transportation and it seldom serves as one's residence or as the repository of personal effects. A car has little capacity for escaping public scrutiny. It travels public thoroughfares where both its occupants and its contents are in plain view. (p. 590)

In *Cardwell*, police arrested an individual for murder and then towed his car to the impoundment lot. To connect the vehicle to the murder scene but without a warrant, officers collected paint scrapings and tire prints. The Court determined that this search did not violate constitutional standards.

Introducing the expectation of privacy into the automobile exception produced some confusion about the warrantless searches of containers within vehicles. Three examples are the search of a locked footlocker, *United States v. Chadwick* (1977); a suitcase, *Arkansas v. Sanders* (1979); and objects wrapped in green opaque plastic, *Robbins v. California* (1981). The Court disallowed each of these searches based on the owner's expectation of privacy, even though each container was inside an automobile and police had probable cause to search the vehicle or to believe that a container held contraband.

The Supreme Court resolved this confusion in *United States v. Ross* (1982), deciding that "the scope of a warrantless search of an automobile is not defined by the nature of the container . . . but by the object of the search and the places in which there is probable cause to believe it may be found" (p. 824). In *Ross*, the Court upheld the search of a closed brown paper bag in a trunk based on a known informant's tip that the driver was selling drugs from his trunk. This ruling was expanded in *California v. Acevedo* (1991), in which the Court decided that the automobile exception applies even when probable cause extends only to specific closed containers (in *Acevedo*, a brown paper bag containing marijuana) and not to the automobile itself. Overall, warrantless searches of automobiles and the items inside do not run afoul of the Fourth Amendment when justified by probable cause and when any portions of the vehicle or any closed containers inside reasonably could hold what is being searched for by law enforcement.

New issues will arise as technology improves and questions about what constitutes a search emerge. For example, in cases that involve surveillance rather than searching vehicle interiors, the Supreme Court has required search warrants for attaching GPS devices to vehicles, *United States v. Jones* (2012), and for accessing cell site location data from wireless carriers, *Carpenter v. United States* (2018). Defining both types of surveillance as searches, the Court has declined to include either in the automobile exception.

About the author

Melinda Gann Hall is a professor at Michigan State University. Her research focuses on state supreme courts, judicial decision-making, and judicial selection.

Suggestions for further reading

In this book
See essays 48 (Homes and the Fourth Amendment) and 53 (Why Do Courts Throw Out Good Evidence?).

Elsewhere
United States v. Jones, 565 U.S. 400 (2012).

50

Electronic Surveillance and Tracking

Tinsley Griffin Hill

Sometimes it seems as though we live in a world of science fiction: we use facial recognition software on our phones, our fingerprints unlock databases, and we can exchange money in milliseconds without ever opening a wallet. However, these scientific achievements generate a wealth of information that can potentially invade a person's privacy. With the creation of new technology, judges and legislators have been scrambling to develop rules that balance public safety with personal privacy. What right does the government have to track you? To listen in on your conversations? To hack your private messages in the interest of public safety?

Many people would like to believe private data is protected from the government—our private health information, the videos we watch, the people we talk to, and so on. Americans tend to be individualists, and freedom is very dear to us. Protection of absolute privacy may better preserve freedom, but protecting private data has costs. This is particularly true in criminal law: for example, if a known terrorist is planning an attack, would it not be helpful for the government to track their location? Do we want the government to keep track of internet searches that imply someone is making a bomb? Should prosecutors be able to use private text messages (obtained without a warrant) as evidence in criminal court?

Social media platforms may not have been around for very long, but the use of technology in law enforcement is not a new topic of study. The Supreme Court first addressed these in *Olmstead v. U.S.* (1928) when police officers wiretapped a bootlegger's phone so they could listen to his phone conversations and track his criminal activity. In that case, the court held that if there was no physical examination of private property, there was no invasion of privacy. This case has since been overturned but first formed the question, Under what conditions do the needs of law enforcement outweigh privacy interests in keeping electronic data confidential?

A right to data privacy is not explicitly mentioned in the Constitution, but the Fourth Amendment prohibits the government from searching or taking your property without a search warrant issued by a judge. This leaves courts to decide what counts as a "search" and what "property" is protected. The Founding Fathers didn't talk about internet search histories, but the Fourth Amendment does refer to people's "houses, papers, and effects." The Supreme Court has decided that the Constitution implies there are areas of your life that are private and has interpreted the Fourth Amendment to protect electronic information, in at least some circumstances.

In *Katz v. United States* (1967), federal agents wiretapped a phone booth, hoping to gain evidence on a local gambling ring. The Supreme Court overturned the earlier case and decided that the Fourth Amendment created a right to privacy in conversations—one justice famously said that it was created to protect "people, not places." The *Katz* decision was a large step toward greater protection for data privacy.

After the 9/11 terrorist attacks, Congress passed the USA PATRIOT Act. This act increased the government's ability to track and monitor anyone whom they suspected of being involved in terrorist activities. Before the act, the government had to gain search warrants to access most private information. Using authority granted in the USA PATRIOT Act, the FBI has collected, without search warrants, logs of text messages, phone calls, and visitors to websites. These searches have not often been challenged in court, because the evidence uncovered has rarely been used in criminal prosecutions.

One trail of data generated by modern technology is the location tracking by cell phones. Timothy Carpenter was suspected of perpetrating a string of robberies. Police obtained from his cell phone service company months of location data. These data revealed where Carpenter slept and attended church. After being convicted for the robberies, Carpenter asserted that by collecting this information, the government had violated his rights under the Fourth Amendment. In *Carpenter v. United States* (2018), the Supreme Court agreed, ruling that the government cannot access this data without a search warrant.

Another controversy involves whether police can access data stored on a person's smartphone without a search warrant. A California court ruled in 2019 that fingerprint access to phones is protected from police search, but courts in Illinois and Minnesota have disagreed, ruling that only a passcode, not facial recognition or fingerprint access, is protected from government access. So far, the Supreme Court has not made a decision on this issue, but as the states continue to disagree, the Court may take up the case in the future.

Where does this leave us? The Fourth Amendment protects personal privacy, and the Supreme Court has found that this protection extends to electronic communications and records, at least in some circumstances. But this information is very useful to law enforcement: quick access to information could prevent school shootings and terrorist attacks. Law enforcement agencies probably collect more electronic information than they acknowledge, and this collection is often only revealed if the target is put on trial. All we can say for now is that the Constitution does protect electronic records in some situations, but the scope of that protection is likely to change over time with new developments in technology and evolving perspectives on the appropriate balance of personal privacy and public safety.

About the author

Tinsley Griffin Hill is a political scientist and litigation attorney in Birmingham, Alabama, and was the first female graduate of the JD/PhD program at the University of Alabama. Her research primarily focuses on state and local courts.

Suggestions for further reading

In this book
See essays 48 (Homes and the Fourth Amendment), 49 (Automobiles and the Fourth Amendment), and 53 (Why Do Courts Throw Out Good Evidence?).

Elsewhere
Cayford, Michelle, and Wolter Pieters. 2018. "The Effectiveness of Surveillance Technology: What Intelligence Officials Are Saying." *Information Society* 24 (2): 88–103.

Hu, Margaret. 2018. "Cybersurveillance Intrusions and an Evolving Katz Privacy Test." *American Criminal Law Review* 55 (1): 127–53.

Carpenter v. United States, 585 U.S. 2018 (2018).

51
Taking the Fifth

David E. Klein

As an enterprising junior member of a crime syndicate, Jack has participated in numerous abductions and assaults. At his boss's criminal trial, he is asked whether his boss ever directed him to perform a criminal act. Jack invokes his Fifth Amendment right not to answer the question, and the judge allows him to leave the stand without answering it.

Jordan is called as a witness at the same trial. He is an engineer who has never participated in any serious criminal activity but had a brief affair with the crime boss. Jordan desperately wishes to keep his wife and children from learning about the affair and wants to avoid being publicly linked to a crime figure. So he too invokes his Fifth Amendment right not to answer. The judge informs Jordan that he has no such right in this situation and orders him to answer the question.

To readers familiar with the self-incrimination clause, the difference in outcomes might not seem strange. But it really should. In our hypotheticals, the person who has done much more harm to society and whose testimony would be much more valuable for securing a conviction is allowed to avoid testifying. The person whose offense was against his spouse, not society, and whose testimony matters less for the prosecution, is forced to testify, at great personal cost to himself and others.

Why these odd results? They arise from Supreme Court interpretations of the clause that, in some cases, have expanded its reach; in others, have narrowed its scope; and in almost every case, have been reasoned and reasonable.

Before going any further, we need to recognize that regardless of what most of us call the clause, the term "incrimination" doesn't actually appear in it. What the Fifth Amendment says is that no person "shall be compelled in any criminal case to be a witness against himself."

This language could easily be read to mean that we are only protected from testifying against ourselves at our own criminal trials. But the Supreme Court has decisively rejected this narrow reading. We can invoke the right to remain silent any time we're under oath—say, in a civil trial or a legislative hearing—and even when we're being questioned by the police (see the next essay in this volume, on Miranda warnings). What matters is not in what forum authorities are compelling us to testify but whether those authorities could use what we're saying to aid in a criminal prosecution against us. That's why Jack could invoke the Fifth Amendment even at someone else's trial.

Why couldn't Jordan invoke the clause at the same trial? Because while the Court has taken an expansive view of *where* the clause applies, it has taken a narrow view of *what* it guards against. It does not protect us against revealing things that could humiliate us, cost us money, or even put us in grave danger. (For instance, if the crime boss had threatened to kill Jordan if he admitted their affair, Jordan would still not have a constitutional right to refuse to testify.) It only protects us against revealing things that could help convict us of a crime or secure a higher sentence after a conviction.

In criminal constitutional law, the individual's loss is usually society's gain. The benefits to society of interpreting "witness against himself" narrowly may not be obvious in Jordan's case (How does society benefit from a wrecked marriage?), but they are readily apparent in the next stage of Jack's story.

Fearing that their case against the crime boss isn't sufficiently convincing, the prosecutors decide they must get Jack to testify about the illegal acts he has performed at the boss's direction. How can the prosecutors accomplish this? If Jack himself has been charged with a crime, they might use that leverage to gain his cooperation through a plea agreement. For instance, they might promise that if Jack pleads guilty to one charge and testifies, they will request a reduced sentence and drop other charges against him. But even if they lack that leverage or he refuses a deal, prosecutors have a more powerful tool at their disposal. They can obtain a court order that grants Jack immunity—a binding promise not to prosecute him for a particular offense or, more commonly, not to use his testimony or evidence derived from that testimony against him in a prosecution. Jack cannot refuse this immunity. And because once immunity is granted, his words can no longer put him in jeopardy of conviction, he loses his Fifth Amendment right not to testify. As was the case with Jordan, it doesn't matter that Jack fears violent retaliation from his boss and doesn't want his family to know what he has been up to.

Of course, through immunity, Jack receives something valuable in return for being forced to testify, which is more than Jordan can say. This disparity in treatment, the necessity for the prosecution to have special tools to compel testimony, and the power of those tools all flow from the

Supreme Court's simultaneously broad and narrow readings of the self-incrimination clause.

About the author

David E. Klein is a professor of political science at Eastern Michigan University. His work focuses primarily on judicial decision-making and the development of the law.

Suggestions for further reading

In this book
See essays 31 (Does the Constitution Protect the Right to Lie?) and 52 (Police Interrogations and the Miranda Warnings).

Elsewhere
Kastigar v. United States, 406 U.S. 441 (1972): Immunity.

Mitchell v. United States, 526 U.S. 314 (1999): Privilege against self-incrimination at the sentencing phase of the trial.

U.S. Department of Justice policy on plea agreements:

- https://www.justice.gov/jm/jm-9-27000-principles-federal -prosecution#9-27.600
- https://www.justice.gov/jm/jm-9-27000-principles-federal -prosecution#9-27.410

52
Police Interrogations and the Miranda Warnings

Ryan J. Williams

The camera pans to a suspect, fear in his eyes. He has been arrested on suspicion of murder and placed in an interview room for questioning by police detectives. When the detectives enter the room, the suspect asks for an attorney. One of the detectives says they'll call the lawyer in a while after the suspect answers a few questions. When the suspect keeps his mouth shut, the detectives slam him up against a wall, demanding he confess. This strategy doesn't work, so the other detective lies to the suspect, saying that the suspect's friend has testified that the suspect is guilty.

Although such treatment by the police is still commonplace on television, it is less common in real police interrogations than it was before several key twentieth-century Supreme Court decisions. These include *Brown v. Mississippi* (1936) and *Spano v. New York* (1959), in which the Court ruled that using torture or other forms of intense coercion to obtain confessions violates the Fourteenth Amendment's due process clause. However, the most important decision by far was *Miranda v. Arizona* (1966).

In *Miranda*, the Court ruled that the Fifth and Sixth Amendments provide protections for criminal suspects beyond prohibiting physical and psychological coercion and that suspects must be made aware of these protections. The Fifth Amendment provides that "no person . . . shall be compelled in any criminal case to be a witness against himself." You might be familiar with this right in the context of criminal trials, where a criminal defendant may "plead the fifth" to avoid giving testimony that may damage their case. Since *Miranda*, the protection against self-incrimination has also applied to our choice to remain silent during a police interrogation and refuse to give information that may advance the criminal case against us.

An important part of this protection is the right to have a lawyer present during the interrogation, especially to protect suspects against the police trying to coerce a confession. Indeed, once a police investigation has turned from a general search to focus on a specific suspect, the Sixth Amendment right to an attorney applies not only to trials before a judge or jury but during all phases of the criminal justice process, including during initial police interrogations (*Escobedo v. Illinois* [1964]). Further, once a suspect asks for an attorney, police are not allowed to keep questioning them, and any incriminating statements that a suspect makes without an attorney there cannot be used in a criminal trial.

Crucially, the Court also held that protecting suspects from self-incrimination requires police to be more than passive bystanders who assume individuals will know their rights. Instead, police must play an active role in informing individuals of their rights. Here's where the well-known Miranda rights come in. Although there is no official, standardized script—each state determines what its officers should say—the warnings have the following general four-part form:

> You have the right to remain silent. Anything you say can and will be used against you in a court of law. You have the right to an attorney. If you cannot afford an attorney, the state will provide you one.

In general, suspects in police custody must be given these warnings before interrogation begins. Suspects are usually asked to acknowledge that they have been read their Miranda rights through verbal or written confirmation.

The *Miranda* decision acknowledged that law enforcement has more power than criminal suspects, and it tried to level the playing field. This case is an important product of the "Warren Court," an era of the 1950s and '60s in which the Supreme Court, led by Chief Justice Earl Warren, emphasized protecting the rights of criminal defendants more than in any other period in the Court's history.

The *Miranda* decision has met with controversy from the beginning. Three justices wrote dissenting opinions in the case expressing their concern with the Court's ruling. For example, in his dissent, Justice Tom Clarke wrote that the decision went too far in its interpretation of the Fifth Amendment and would make it difficult for police officers to fulfill their duties.

Such criticisms led to Supreme Court decisions that have carved out a number of exceptions to the *Miranda* ruling. There's an exception where a suspect's answers to police questions that are aimed at removing a danger to public safety may be used in court even if no Miranda warning was given (*New York v. Quarles* [1984]). There's an exception for when a suspect only vaguely mentions wanting an attorney present (*Davis v. United States* [1994]). And there's an exception for suspects who remain silent but don't explicitly say that they're invoking that right (*Berghuis v. Thompkins* [2010]). These exceptions have led some scholars and pundits to question whether the decision adequately protects Fifth Amendment rights.

As one of the Supreme Court's most cited precedents, *Miranda* occupies an important place in the American public consciousness. While the Supreme Court has never directly overruled it, Supreme Court decisions of the last several decades have shifted power from criminal suspects to law enforcement. Many suspects actually waive their Miranda rights in police custody. While brutal coercion techniques are less common nowadays, more subtle interrogation techniques, combined with a weakened set of *Miranda* rights, raise important questions about the role of self-incrimination protections today.

About the author

Ryan J. Williams is an assistant professor of political science and criminal justice at the University of South Alabama. His work focuses on U.S. judicial politics, criminal justice, and teaching and learning in the political science classroom.

Suggestions for further reading

In this book
See essays 51 (Taking the Fifth) and 53 (Why Do Courts Throw Out Good Evidence?).

Elsewhere
Cortner, Richard C. 1986. *A Scottsboro Case in Mississippi: The Supreme Court and Brown v. Mississippi*. Jackson: University of Mississippi Press.

Peabody, Bruce. 2016. "Fifty Years Later, the Miranda Decision Hasn't Accomplished What the Supreme Court Intended." *Monkey Cage* (blog), *Washington Post*. June 13, 2016. https://www.washingtonpost.com/news/monkey-cage/wp/2016/06/13/your-miranda-rights-are-50-years-old-today-heres-how-that-decision-has-aged/.

53
Why Do Courts Throw Out Good Evidence?

Wendy L. Martinek

Courts throw out good evidence when that evidence has been obtained in ways that conflict with constitutional protections for those suspected or accused of crimes. This is known as the exclusionary rule. For example, the Fourth Amendment provides protection against unreasonable searches and seizures. With some exceptions, this means that the search of a home requires a search warrant issued by a judge based on a finding of probable cause that evidence of a crime will be found at that home. If the police enter and search a home without a search warrant and find evidence of a crime, then that evidence is likely to be excluded from use at trial.

The exclusionary rule governs the conduct of the criminal justice process. Like other procedural rules, it is intended to ensure fairness. The idea is that requiring all parties to follow the same rules will make it more likely for a trial verdict to be correct—that is, result in the conviction of the guilty and the exoneration of the innocent. However, the evidence challenged under the exclusionary rule almost always points toward guilt. (A person accused of a crime will not want to exclude evidence that supports a finding of not guilty!) The consequence of this imbalance is that the application of the exclusionary rule makes arriving at a correct trial verdict less likely.

There is no language in the Constitution that explicitly creates the exclusionary rule. The Supreme Court fashioned this rule through its interpretation of the Fourth Amendment in *Weeks v. United States* (1914). The Court's reasoning was that a court had no authority to enter evidence at trial if that evidence was obtained in violation of the constitutional rights of the criminally accused. Over time, particularly after Chief Justice Warren Burger (a critic of the exclusionary rule) took office, the Court began to frame the exclusionary rule differently. Instead of considering exclusion a constitutional right belonging to a criminal defendant, the Court began to focus on its ability to deter unconstitutional police behavior. The Court established an explicit cost-benefit analysis in *United States v. Calandra* (1974). In this analysis, the Court assesses the likelihood that improper police behavior will be deterred in the future through exclusion of the evidence in this case. It only excludes the evidence if it believes the benefits of deterrence outweigh the societal costs of letting a guilty person go free.

When it originated, the exclusionary rule did not prevent law enforcement from using unconstitutionally obtained evidence as the starting point for finding additional evidence of a crime. This meant that, though the original evidence may have been tainted (and, therefore, barred from use at trial under the exclusionary rule), any subsequent evidence found because of that original, unconstitutionally obtained evidence was not automatically subject to exclusion at trial. The Court eliminated that loophole in *Silverthorne Lumber Company v. United States* (1920), initiating what later became known as the fruit of the poisonous tree doctrine: if the original source (the "tree") is tainted, then the subsequent evidence (the "fruit") is also tainted.

There are exceptions to the fruit of the poisonous tree doctrine. One exception occurs when the police have another independent source of information leading to the evidence. For example, if the police find documents detailing an illegal pyramid scheme through an unwarranted search of a home, that evidence is likely to be excluded at trial. But if the police also receive copies of those documents from a reliable, confidential source, then the exclusionary rule most likely will not be applied. Another exception occurs when the evidence found through unconstitutional means would inevitably have been discovered through other means. For example, if law enforcement finds clues about an illegal drug operation through an unwarranted search of a home and then goes to the location and collects evidence of the drug operation, that evidence is likely to be excluded at trial. But if the location of the drug operation is easily accessible to the public and little effort has been put into hiding the illegal activities, then the evidence is no longer poisoned fruit because it would most likely have been found even in the absence of the clues from the unconstitutional search.

The U.S. Supreme Court did not make the Fourth Amendment apply to the states until its decision in *Wolf v. Colorado* (1949). In that case, the Court found that the due process protections included in the Fourteenth Amendment (which applied directly to the states) meant that the states, too, were barred from unreasonable searches and seizures. But the Court did not require the states to throw out good evidence to address violations of that protected right. The Court suggested that there were other ways that states could do that, including relying on internal police disciplinary procedures or civil suits. After more than a decade of experience demonstrating how unworkable alternative means of enforcing the Fourth Amendment were, the Court reversed itself and made the exclusionary rule mandatory for states in its decision in *Mapp v. Ohio* (1961).

About the author

Wendy L. Martinek is a professor of political science at Binghamton University. She works primarily on judicial decision-making and the design of courts.

Suggestions for further reading

In this book
See essays 48–50 (on search and seizure) and 52 (Police Interrogations and the Miranda Warnings).

Elsewhere
Gless, Sabine, and Thomas Richter, eds. 2019. *Do Exclusionary Rules Ensure a Fair Trial? A Comparative Perspective on Evidentiary Rules*. New York: Springer.

Long, Carolyn N. 2006. *Mapp v. Ohio: Guarding against Unreasonable Searches and Seizures*. Lawrence: University Press of Kansas.

National Constitution Center. 2021. "The Fourth Amendment and Policing in America, Featuring Charles Ramsey." Last modified May 7, 2021. https://constitutioncenter.org/education/videos/the-fourth-amendment -and-policing-in-america-featuring-charles-ramsey.

54

Cruel and Unusual Punishments

Taneisha N. Means

> Excessive bail shall not be required, nor excessive fines imposed,
> nor cruel and unusual punishments inflicted.
> —U.S. Constitution, Eighth Amendment

The Eighth Amendment was adopted with the rest of the Bill of Rights in 1791, but its origins can be traced back to the 1689 English Bill of Rights. It is designed to guard against the use of government-sanctioned punishments as tools of oppression. The amendment makes clear that fines and bail amounts should be in proportion to the crimes committed. However, its vague reference to "cruel and unusual punishments" has generated many questions.

Most fundamentally, people disagree about the standards courts should use to determine whether punishments are cruel and unusual. Some object to using present-day values because they see it as at odds with the rule of law. These individuals believe the standards should be the ones that existed in 1791. Others believe that contemporary practices and understandings of what is decent and acceptable should help us determine the meaning of cruel and unusual.

The Supreme Court has leaned toward the latter position. In *Weems v. United States* (1910), the Court wrote that "a principle, to be vital, must be capable of wider application than the mischief which gave it birth. This is peculiarly true of constitutions." It held that a fifteen-year sentence involving forced labor and shackling from wrist to ankle was cruel and unusual for the crime of falsifying court documents with intent to defraud the government. In *Trop v. Dulles* (1958), invalidating a sentence that stripped a wartime deserter of citizenship, the Court said that the Eighth Amendment "must draw its meaning from the evolving standards of decency that mark the progress of a maturing society."

Courts since have made frequent reference to "evolving standards" when assessing whether specific punishments are cruel and unusual. As a result, defendants and inmates have won some new protections, although courts reject a large majority of their claims.

In 1972 (*Furman v. Georgia*), a majority of the Court held that the death penalty was unconstitutional, at least as it was applied at the time. But in 1976, the Court allowed the death penalty to go forward, with new guidelines for deciding when a death sentence may be imposed (*Gregg v. Georgia, Woodson v. North Carolina*). Since then, the Court has set only a few new limits regarding the people subject to the death penalty and the manner in which it is carried out.

Incarceration is a far less controversial punishment than execution, and courts typically hand down sentences in proportion to the severity of the crimes. But what happens when they do not? Is a punishment that is disproportionate to the crime cruel and unusual? The Supreme Court's answer is "not necessarily." It has held that the Constitution does not require strict proportionality between crimes and sentences; a sentence is only unconstitutional if it is "grossly disproportionate" to the crime. In a key case, *Harmelin v. Michigan* (1991), the Court permitted the imposition of a life sentence without the possibility of parole for the possession of a substantial amount of cocaine.

The absence of a strict proportionality guarantee has been especially important for "three-strikes laws." These laws were born out of states' desires to get tougher on habitual offenders and reduce recidivism. They require long prison terms for individuals convicted of any felony if they have previously been convicted of two or more serious crimes. In *Ewing v. California* (2003) and *Lockyer v. Andrade* (2003), individuals convicted of shoplifting were sentenced to a minimum of twenty-five years in prison under three-strikes laws. Although recognizing that these were very long sentences for rather minor crimes, viewed in isolation, the Supreme Court held that they were not grossly disproportionate once the defendants' records of recidivism were taken into account.

Incarcerated persons in the United States regularly experience over-crowding, excessive and extended solitary confinement, limited food options, lack of access to proper clothing, and the denial of mental health and medical care. Moreover, inmates are constantly exposed to violence from other inmates. Of course, incarceration is meant to be a punishment. Some people argue that harsh prison conditions are unavoidable and, in fact, might deter people from engaging in criminal activities. Others, however, maintain that prisoners are entitled to maintain their human dignity despite their imprisonment and that prison and jail officials violate the Constitution if they fail to protect inmates' health and safety and provide decent living conditions.

Courts have steered something of a middle course between these positions. They have held that inmates have a constitutional right to, and cannot be deprived of, "the basic necessities of life, which include reasonably adequate food, clothing, shelter, sanitation, and necessary medical attention" (*Newman v. State of Alabama* [1977]). Furthermore, prison officers may not deliberately, "maliciously and sadistically" use force to significantly injure inmates (*Hudson v. McMillian* [1992]). Applying these principles, courts have sometimes intervened in dramatic ways in prison operations; for example, in 2011 (*Brown v. Plata*), the Supreme Court upheld a lower court decision ordering California to reduce its prison population by forty-six thousand people. However, courts have not recognized the kind of broad, sweeping constitutional protections that inmate advocates would like to see.

The *purported* function of the criminal justice system is to protect society from crime. But as the Eighth Amendment reminds us, it also must provide protection for those who are accused of crimes, even the guilty. As long as we have crime, we will face the challenge of drawing lines, not just between just and unduly harsh punishments, but between constitutional and unconstitutional punishments.

About the author

Taneisha N. Means is an assistant professor of political science on the Class of 1951 Chair at Vassar College in Poughkeepsie, New York. Her primary research interests are at the intersection of racial and ethnic politics and judicial politics, and she is primarily concerned with the level, nature, and significance of racial and gender diversity in state courts.

Suggestions for further reading

In this book
See essay 6 (How Can We Tell What the Constitution Means?).

Elsewhere
Lockyer v. Andrade, 538 U.S. 63 (2003).

Roper v. Simmons, 543 U.S. 551 (2005): Death penalty for a crime committed by someone under eighteen.

Looking Outward
and Forward

55
The U.S. Constitution as an International Model

Monica Lineberger

Reflecting on the still-young Constitution in 1802, Thomas Jefferson remarked, "It is impossible not to sense that we are acting for all mankind." The writers of the Constitution had themselves believed that the words and ideas enshrined in the document would have a major impact on other nations. Was this an example of unfounded pride, or were the founders right to think the Constitution would be so influential?

The first indication that the founders were right came quickly, as French revolutionaries turned to the new United States as a model for how to design a government where people were at the helm of power. The U.S. Bill of Rights and Declaration of Independence were sources of inspiration for the French Declaration of the Rights of Man. In fact, the drafters of the Declaration of the Rights of Man consulted with Thomas Jefferson on the rights that would be included.

Why did the French revolutionaries rely so heavily upon these American resources? After all, the Magna Carta of 1215 and the English Bill of Rights from 1689 had been enacted years earlier and had themselves influenced the U.S. Bill of Rights.

Though the U.S. Bill of Rights was not the first document to enshrine the rights of the people, it was significant because of its inclusion in a constitution. The U.S. Constitution was the first example of how citizens could create a nation by laying out its structure in a single document. Previously, countries would pass laws dictating how the government should function. But these laws could be repealed or rewritten just as easily as they had been passed. The U.S. Constitution was placed on a higher plane than ordinary legislation: not only is it designated "the supreme Law of the Land," but it may only be amended by supermajorities of both houses of Congress and of the states.

198 THE U.S. CONSTITUTION IN FIVE MINUTES

The demanding amendment process provides continuity and stability. A Polish constitution written just four years later agreed about the need to avoid "abrupt and frequent changes of the national constitution." Although many countries have made their constitutions easier to amend than the U.S. Constitution, the principle that constitutions should be harder to change than ordinary legislation is widely accepted.

The U.S. Constitution has not only served as a model for establishing a durable governmental system through a foundational document; it also influenced other countries' specific design choices. Key features of the Constitution—such as the separation of powers, federalism, and presidentialism—are still popular ways to construct government. More than 55 percent of constitutions in 2020 use the presidential system, though with their own variations. While the federal system was not an American invention, originally inspired by the Iroquois Confederacy, 62 percent of constitutions formally recognize a subnational unit, and many adopt similar principles that attempt to balance power between national and regional governments.

One minor aspect of the Constitution that has been surprisingly influential is the adoption of minimum age requirements for political officials. Of the constitutions that specify a minimum age for political offices, about 30 percent have adopted one or more of the specific age requirements from the U.S. Constitution.

However, if I were to ask you how you view the Constitution, you probably would not immediately think of these structural elements. You might reflect on its symbolic power. Or you might note how it represents the best (political freedoms) and worst (institutionalized slavery) of America. Whatever you consider, you likely have fairly strong feelings about this legal document. Because it's not just a framework for a system of government. It's also an expression of American symbols and ideals.

These ideals were put into words in the preamble, the short paragraph at the beginning of the Constitution. The principles and symbols embedded in the preamble have been replicated in other constitutions all over the world. Perhaps the most fundamental symbol the Constitution represents is that of self-government.

The first three words of the U.S. Constitution, "We the People," designate the citizens as the sovereign, not the states or a monarch. This expressive statement within the preamble to the Constitution has been one of its major influences upon other constitutions. "We the People" is the most popular phrase within the preambles of constitutions worldwide. About 25 percent of constitutions written since 1990 imported the phrase.

The expressive value of the preamble itself has also been popular worldwide. Since 1787, 80 percent of constitutions contain preambles. They, like the one used in the United States, express the identity of the country and clarify the purpose of the constitution. In fact, of the constitutions adopted after 2003, the Maldives is the only country to not include a preamble.

Our Constitution was the first of its kind. It laid out a structure of government that provided power and rights to the people, created a system of separation of powers, and placed intention behind who should hold office. Its impact was immediate and continual. It inspired contemporary constitutions created in Europe in the 1790s, but it has also acted as a model for other former colonies creating a national government throughout the 1900s and for new democracies in the twenty-first century. While some particularities of the system are outdated—the Electoral College, for one—its structure and significance still influence constitutional design worldwide.

About the author

Monica Lineberger is an assistant professor of political science at the University of Wisconsin-Whitewater. Her research examines comparative judicial behavior and the institutional design of common law courts.

Suggestions for further reading

In this book
See essays 1 (Why Do We Have a Constitution?), 5 (Emulation and Innovation in the Constitutional System), and 56 (Different Approaches to National Constitutions).

Elsewhere
Billias, George Athan. 2009. *American Constitutionalism Heard round the World, 1776–1989: A Global Perspective*. New York: New York University Press.

Constitute Project website. http://constituteproject.org.

Elkins, Zachary, Tom Ginsburg, and James Melton. 2009. *The Endurance of National Constitutions*. New York: Cambridge University Press.

56
Different Approaches to National Constitutions

Matthew Reid Krell

> If I were writing a constitution in 2012, I wouldn't look to the United States.
>
> —Ruth Bader Ginsburg

The American constitutional order represents an earlier era. The oldest still-active written national constitution, the 1789 American Constitution is a shift from everything that had come before it and thus exerted tremendous influence over constitution-making in the eighteenth and early nineteenth centuries. However, as time went on and lessons were learned from the American experiment and its imitators, constitution writers began to look elsewhere for ideas. By the early twenty-first century, the United States had become an outlier in global democratic constitutions in structure, powers, and the protection of fundamental rights.

Government Structure

The American constitutional order is widely recognized as creating three constitutional innovations in the structure of government. The first is federalism, where the central government shares power with subunits. The second is presidentialism, where the head of the executive branch is elected separately from the legislature and has an independent role in the lawmaking process. Finally, American courts innovated judicial review, where courts can have the final word on whether validly enacted laws are constitutional, and if not, to declare them void. However, none of these structures are common today.

Federalism has never been especially popular as an organizing structure. The peak of federal states was achieved at less than 25 percent of countries in the world, immediately in the wake of the breakup of the Russian Empire in the early twentieth century. While intermediate, devolved structures are not uncommon, as in the United Kingdom, significant power in the subunits is only held right now in about fifteen countries. The cause of this may be that American-style federalism probably requires the creation of a central government from smaller units with unique identities and interests. This may explain why federalism in the American style, where the Constitution enumerates separate spheres of power for national and subunit governments, is only present in Australia, Canada, India, and Germany, with some scholars also listing Switzerland and Guyana.

The American-style presidency was imitated throughout Latin America as Spain and France withdrew from their colonial empires through the nineteenth century. But unlawful seizures of executive power are significantly more likely in presidential systems than the alternatives, and Latin American presidential systems proved to be unstable. Thus, most constitution-making since World War II has either followed a parliamentary system like the "Westminster" democracies that follow the United Kingdom's example or semipresidential systems like France or Poland, where the president shares executive authority with a prime minister the legislature chooses.

While American courts created the power of judicial review in the case of *Hylton v. United States* and first exercised it in *Marbury v. Madison*, American-style judicial review, where any court can review the constitutionality of a law, is relatively rare. Far more common is for a specialized court to hear questions of constitutionality, using a model designed by legal theorist Hans Kelsen in Czechoslovakia in 1920. Between these two poles, there is substantial variation, including Israel's creation of a special judicial review court that is made up of the same judges as the Supreme Court, Russia's grant of power to ordinary courts to resolve constitutional questions but only binding the parties to a case, and the Canadian "notwithstanding" clause, which allows the legislature to override a judicial determination that a law is unconstitutional. American-style judicial review, where any judge can declare a law unconstitutional for the entire country, may be too chaotic for many constitution-makers. In fact, the United States has had situations where litigants seeking to declare a particular policy unconstitutional would seek out a friendly judge.

Fundamental Rights

The American Constitution is regarded as an outlier in protecting fundamental human rights. There are sixty fundamental rights that have constitutional status somewhere in the world, with the average constitution listing thirty-four of them. The American Constitution protects twenty-one of them. The American Constitution protects an individual's right to bear arms, a right that exists in only two other constitutions worldwide, Guatemala and Mexico. Only about a third of democratic constitutions provide for a separation of church and state as the American Constitution does. The American Constitution does not protect its own democratic nature, as American courts have found that the Constitution's guarantee of a "republican form of government" is unenforceable except by Congress, which has only taken such action once. And the American Constitution does not provide an affirmative right to vote.

The unenumerated rights doctrine is an important source of American constitutional rights, ranging from the right to access birth control to the right to travel across state lines. However, unenumerated rights only form part of the constitutional structure in three other countries with written constitutions—Australia, Ireland, and Taiwan. Arguably, the United Kingdom also has an unenumerated rights doctrine, but since its development predates American colonization, it's difficult to describe it as a place where the American system has influenced the law.

Instead, constitution-makers in modern times tend to look beyond the American Constitution for fundamental liberties sources. The most common source of influence is the Canadian Charter of Rights and Freedoms. While some scholars also recommend that the postapartheid South African constitution and the European Convention on Human Rights serve as sources, there's little indication of global influence for either of these documents.

Conclusion

Ultimately, the American Constitution reflects the time in which it was made. It was a tremendous leap forward from the monarchical and personalist systems in place in the late eighteenth century and has proven flexible enough to support an evolving and innovating society for almost 250 years. But because it retains so much of its eighteenth-century character and does not reflect modern understandings of the role and scope of government, its ability to influence other countries' constitutions is waning, and the American constitutional order is becoming more and more out of step with the global consensus.

About the author

Matthew Reid Krell is a visiting assistant professor of law at Washburn University School of Law in Topeka, Kansas. His research focuses on the politics of procedure and litigant behavior across multiple contexts.

Suggestions for further reading

In this book
See essays 5 (Emulation and Innovation in the Constitutional System) and 55 (The U.S. Constitution as an International Model).

Elsewhere
Billias, George Athan. 2009. *American Constitutionalism Heard round the World, 1776–1989: A Global Perspective.* New York: New York University Press.

Law, David, and Mila Versteeg. 2012. "The Declining Influence of the American Constitution." *New York University Law Review* 87:762.

Sabato, Larry. 2008. *A More Perfect Constitution: Why the Constitution Must Be Revised: Ideas to Inspire a New Generation.* New York: Bloomsbury USA.

57

Does the Constitution Work in a Crisis?

David Crockett

A common complaint about the Constitution is that it is an eighteenth-century document confronting twenty-first-century problems. The implication is that a document drafted in a horse-and-buggy era—before electrical outlets, airliners, and nuclear weapons—cannot possibly be equipped to handle contemporary emergencies. Most critically, how can we expect the Constitution to enable public officials to address the ravages of a swiftly moving global pandemic, a stock market crash that leads to an economic collapse, or a surprise attack planned and projected from halfway around the world? In short—does the Constitution work in a crisis?

Although they were hardly capable of anticipating the speed and lethality of modern warfare, the framers of the Constitution did, in fact, understand the need for the government to respond competently in a crisis. Each of the three branches of government is designed and constructed to provide certain objectives that are necessary if we are to consider republican government to be effective. The primary function of Congress is, in the words of Alexander Hamilton, to "prescribe rules for the regulation of the society," and it is structured to do this by comprising many legislators who represent citizens in different ways, through relatively frequent elections, in a deliberative institution. The primary function of the Court is to protect liberty and individual rights through an adjudication process, and it is structured to do this by being made up of a small body of learned experts who can dispassionately and indifferently interpret the law because they have job security.

That, of course, brings us to the presidency. One of the central goals of the Constitutional Convention was to construct a federal government with the capacity to ensure the security and stability of the nation. Hamilton argues that the function of the executive is "the execution of the laws and the employment of the common strength," and it's the phrase "employment of the common strength" that connects directly to the role of the president as a crisis manager.

As with the other two branches, the presidency was structured by the framers to do precisely this task. Both James Madison and Alexander Hamilton articulated the need for what they called "energy" in government. Madison said, "Energy in government is essential to that security against external and internal danger." Hamilton agreed: energy is "essential to the protection of the community against foreign attacks." In order to make energy more likely, the executive is just one individual. A single executive should avoid the crippling differences of opinion and rivalry that mark plural institutions, like Congress. Instead, it will be able to act with "vigor and expedition," with the qualities of "decision, activity, secrecy, and dispatch."

None of this is to suggest that the president has unlimited power in this area. But the other two branches of government are not structurally equipped to handle crises effectively. The presidency is. One example should suffice to demonstrate this. The greatest national security crisis in recent decades was the 2001 terrorist attacks on 9/11. In the days immediately afterward, all attention focused on chief executives—whether the mayor of New York City, the governor of the state, or the president of the United States. And it was President George W. Bush, from the moment he determined to view the attack from a war perspective, who set the nation on a course to retaliate against al-Qaeda and the Taliban regime in Afghanistan and to take dramatic steps to ensure the future security of the nation. By contrast, when an anthrax attack on Capitol Hill took place days later, the leadership of the two congressional chambers could not agree on a unified response. It is much more difficult for plural institutions to respond swiftly and effectively to crises. Thus, whether the crisis is a national security one, like 9/11, or an economic collapse, like the Great Depression, or a natural disaster, like Hurricane Katrina or the COVID-19 pandemic, the nation turns its eyes to the president.

Of course, there is a significant danger with this executive ability. The larger the crisis, the more power seems to flow to the president, sometimes in ways that stretch constitutional boundaries to the breaking point. It is no accident that the presidents during the nation's greatest crises—the Civil War and the Great Depression—were accused by their enemies of being dictators. Abraham Lincoln augmented the armed forces without congressional authorization, spent unappropriated funds, blockaded Southern ports, proclaimed martial law, and suspended the writ of habeas corpus in selected places. Perhaps more frightening, Franklin Roosevelt's fear that some Japanese Americans might assist a Japanese invasion of the American West Coast led him to transport over a hundred thousand Japanese and Japanese American citizens to internment camps in the desert without due process of law and with no pushback from Congress or the Court. It is safe to say that the balance of liberty and security has been one of the more contested arguments since 9/11.

The framers understood that the ability to respond to genuine crises was an essential feature of republican government, and they constructed the presidency accordingly. The fact that the presidency consists of one person makes it easier for the other branches of government, as well as the voting public, to hold the chief executive accountable for his actions. No one, however, envisioned an endless crisis, and it is when emergency powers seemingly have no beginning or end that we see the greatest strain on the constitutional system. Checks and balances remain important even during times of crisis.

About the author

David Crockett is a professor of political science at Trinity University in San Antonio, Texas. His primary area of research is the American presidency and presidential elections.

Suggestions for further reading

In this book
See essays 13 (What Is the Purpose of the Separation of Powers?), 18 (Can the President Start a War?), and 58 (Does the Constitution Cause Gridlock?).

Elsewhere
The Federalist Papers nos. 37, 70, and 75.

Tulis, Jeffrey K. 1987. *The Rhetorical Presidency*. Princeton, NJ: Princeton University Press.

58
Does the Constitution Cause Gridlock?

Richard L. Pacelle Jr.

What is the most important legislation to come from Congress, survive checks and balances, and escape the veto stamp wielded by the president? Among the candidates for this "hall of fame" would be the Civil Rights Act of 1866, the Social Security Act of 1935, the Civil Rights Act of 1964, the Voting Rights Act of 1965, and the Medicare Act of 1965. In addition to their substantive importance, these laws shared another feature: all took special circumstances, a catastrophe (economic disaster, war), or one-party control of government to be passed. The Civil Rights Act of 1866 needed the Civil War, Reconstruction, and the disenfranchisement of the South to be passed. The Social Security Act was a response to the Great Depression. And it took the assassination of a president and a huge electoral landslide in the subsequent election to pass the Civil Rights Act of 1964 and the Voting Rights Act as well as Medicare.

In normal times, the American political system is marked by gridlock, and many argue that the Constitution is to blame. The framers made a deliberate choice to risk gridlock and stalemate rather than invite tyranny. After successfully declaring independence and fomenting revolution, the neophyte nation had to establish a form of government. The Articles of Confederation was an ineffective response. There was no executive and a weak legislature. The framers ostensibly convened to modify the existing structure but instead opted to create a new form of government.

The framers sought to create a government that was limited in size and scope. They wanted to decentralize government to avoid the concentration of power in too few hands. The goal was to create a government that was strong, but not too strong, and effective, but not too effective. The framers borrowed heavily from political theorists in creating devices for limited government and decentralization: separation of powers, checks and balances, and federalism.

The framers set up an obstacle course that made public policy-making an onerous task. They staggered the terms of the elected officials to provide each branch some insulation from the others and from the unpredictable winds of public opinion. Members of the House of Representatives run every two years. Senators serve six-year terms (and only a third are elected at a time). Presidents fall in between at four years. The consequence of the staggered terms is often divided government, a certain recipe for gridlock. As a result, it is difficult to pass coherent, meaningful public policy in the United States.

The system seems built for gridlock. Our system has created more barriers to the enactment of legislation than almost any other nation. The framers wanted to create a form of government with numerous points of access. But each point of access is also a veto point. To get something passed, you must win at every stage. To defeat something, you only need to win at one stage. It is said that the framers devised the system to force compromise, but with the rise of polarization, gridlock has just intensified.

Consider how a bill becomes a law. The idea must be converted into an issue, and then it must be introduced in Congress. The bill normally starts in a committee, and many face a quiet death at that point. If the proposed legislation survives, it will be reported to the full chamber for consideration. If it passes the House, it is off to the Senate and a similar gamut to negotiate. Under Senate rules, there is an added wrinkle: if the opposition has forty-one votes, it could use a filibuster to defeat a measure that a majority supports. If it passes the Senate, any differences between the two houses must be reconciled. If it survives that, it is off to the desk of the president. The policy that emerges from this process is often cast in vague, general terms and passes the responsibility to unelected bureaucrats and judges. Ultimately, the courts (including the Supreme Court) might reinterpret the provisions or declare them unconstitutional.

Gridlock and the vacuum of power have weakened Congress over time, encouraged presidents to act unilaterally, and enhanced the power of courts and the bureaucracy. The system tends to reward the status quo and the "haves" over the "have-nots." The very words "gridlock" and "stalemate" are almost exclusively seen as negative terms (as is the word "politics"), but it should be noted that supporters of smaller, limited government and those who favor the status quo find gridlock to be an important tool in their efforts to curb federal spending and overreach or retain existing advantages.

Although they revere the Constitution, Americans are often critical of government, the policy process, and the substantive results. Few democracies of this type have survived. Indeed, ours is the longest surviving government of its kind. All others like it have died or been replaced. It is notable that when the United States helps a nation rebuild or replace its existing form of government, it never gives them our system.

About the author

Richard L. Pacelle Jr. is a professor of political science at the University of Tennessee. His research focuses on public law, most notably the Supreme Court and political litigation.

Suggestions for further reading

In this book
See essays 13 (What Is the Purpose of the Separation of Powers?), 25 (Why Do Wyoming and California Have the Same Number of Senators?), and 27 (Can the Constitution Handle Political Parties?).

Elsewhere
Klein, Ezra. 2020. *Why We're So Polarized*. London: Profile Books.

Levinson, Sanford. 2006. *Our Undemocratic Constitution: Where the Constitution Goes Wrong (and How We the People Can Correct It)*. New York: Oxford University Press.

Sabato, Larry. 2008. *A More Perfect Constitution: Why the Constitution Must Be Revised: Ideas to Inspire a New Generation*. New York: Bloomsbury USA.

59
Does the Amendment Process Need Amendment?

Bruce Peabody

Some people have called the U.S. Constitution a "machine that would go of itself"—like a watch that never needs winding. But machines wear out and need updates, patches, and repairs. The people who wrote the Constitution knew it wasn't perfect and would need fixes, which is why the document includes Article V, which explains how it can be amended or changed.

Amending the Constitution involves two stages, proposal and then ratification (or approval). The ratification stage requires three-fourths of the states (thirty-eight out of fifty) to go along. Even though members of Congress have introduced more than eleven thousand proposals to change the Constitution over American history, only twenty-seven amendments have gotten through both stages and been added to our supreme law.

So is the procedure for altering the Constitution too clumsy, difficult, or confusing? Does the amendment process itself need amending?

Changing the U.S. Constitution is hard. Comparing our constitutional amendment procedures to those of other nations reveals that ours is one of the most difficult to change in the world (by one scholar's measure of similar nations, only Yugoslavia's constitution is harder to amend). In addition, it seems to be getting more challenging to pass amendments in recent decades, in part because of deep political divisions between the parties and states. While, on average, the U.S. Constitution has been amended about every eight years, if we take out the Twenty-Seventh Amendment (which had no expiration date and was approved over more than two centuries), no amendment has been ratified for over fifty years.

There are some reasons we might stick with our current system. James Madison, our fourth president and one of the Constitution's most important supporters, argued in favor of the existing amendment process on the grounds that it produced "veneration" or respect for the Constitution, keeping it stable. At over 230 years of age, our Constitution is the oldest in the world, and a majority of the public still expresses strong support for the document. Furthermore, if we can change the Constitution too quickly, we could start seeing it as ordinary legislation that reflects special interests or the shifting policy concerns of an era rather than a common charter or general statement of shared values. This could erode the difference between law and politics and water down what we think of as the most important duties of government and our fundamental rights. The California Constitution, which has been amended over five hundred times, protects people's right to fish along with their right to speak, write, and publish.

Making the U.S. Constitution easier to amend could also make it longer and more complicated. The Alabama Constitution has been amended over eight hundred times and is the longest constitution in the world. Following this model might turn our national Constitution into a complex and technical code rather than a document ordinary citizens can study and understand.

On the other hand, some say that our constitutional amendment process needs to be less demanding so that the Constitution can better reflect the will of the people and our greater belief in democracy in the twenty-first century. The Equal Rights Amendment (ERA), which would have required that equal rights not be "denied or abridged . . . on account of sex," was broadly supported by both houses of Congress, majorities of the public, and presidents from both major parties and was ratified by thirty-five out of fifty states. But it fell three states short of ratification in 1977. Most state constitutions can be amended by simple majorities, many of them through popular processes approved by ordinary voters. Thomas Jefferson wrote that we shouldn't "look at constitutions with sanctimonious reverence" but should instead design our supreme law to fit the needs of each generation.

A related set of arguments holds that the Constitution needs updating. The document was written prior to the internet, before the United States became a nuclear superpower, and at a time when many believed in legal, social, and political inequality (placing Blacks, Native Americans, and women, among others, into subordinate roles). In this view, the high barriers of the amendment process make it hard to bring the Constitution into our new millennium. American state constitutions, and national constitutions across the globe, have been amended thousands of times without obviously unraveling the rule of law or creating political chaos.

Making it easier to amend the Constitution is likely to shift power away from judges and back to elected lawmakers and the people. When judges look at constitutional language that is hundreds of years old, they provide their own interpretations to understand issues like what privacy the Constitution protects or the limits to free speech and presidential power. If the amendment process were changed, Congress, the states, and the people might have more voice in addressing these and other fundamental legal questions.

At the end of the day, it appears unlikely that we will change how we amend the Constitution anytime soon. After all, such a move would require either a new amendment or Constitutional Convention. In our current political climate, where the nation is closely divided between the two major parties (and on many constitutional issues) and where voter distrust of politicians remains high, achieving the votes and support for this move is a rather remote possibility.

About the author

Bruce Peabody is a professor of government and politics at Fairleigh Dickinson University in Madison, New Jersey. His research interests include constitutional law and politics.

Suggestions for further reading

In this book
See essays 22 (Who Can Vote?), 40 (How Did the Civil War Amendments Change the Constitution?), and 58 (Does the Constitution Cause Gridlock?).

Elsewhere
Levinson, Sanford. 2006. *Our Undemocratic Constitution: Where the Constitution Goes Wrong (and How We the People Can Correct It)*. New York: Oxford University Press.

Levinson, Sanford, ed. 1995. *Responding to Imperfection: The Theory and Practice of Constitutional Amendment*. Princeton, NJ: Princeton University Press.

Sullivan, Kathleen. 1996. "Constitutional Constancy: Why Congress Should Cure Itself of Amendment Fever." *Cardozo Law Review* 17:691–704.

Index

www.ingramcontent.com/pod-product-compliance
Lightning Source LLC
Chambersburg PA
CBHW040140270326
41928CB00022B/3276